The Good Little Girls

by

Angela Thirkell

2006

The Angela Thirkell Society

Printed by
The Angela Thirkell Society of North America
PO Box 7109
San Diego, CA 92167

First published 2006
Produced in 1952

Printed in the United States of America by Sabina Krewsun, American Index, El Cajon, CA   619-442-8788

LIBRARY OF CONGRESS
CATALOGING-IN-PUBLICATION DATA

ISBN 0-9768345-1-0 (pbk)

1. Title. The Good Little Girls
2. Author. Angela Thirkell

Introduction

The Angela Thirkell Society is pleased to make available an original Angela Thirkell work, a children's play—*The Good Little Girls*. This work was not published in book form when it was originally written, but was apparently for a stage production by a friend, Valery Hovendon, who had a children's theater. There is no known evidence that Mrs. Thirkell saw the production itself. What we know of this play was contained with the manuscript.

"Member's Circular 73, Hovendon Players Ltd., 65a, Shaftesbury Avenue, W1 (GER. 1681) First Performance "THE GOOD LITTLE GIRLS" by Angela Thirkell, from the stories by Mme de Ségur. Monday, Jan. 11 [th] 1953 until Sunday, Jan. 24th (Thursdays excepted) at 7:30 p.m. with Anthony Bradley, Caroline Comyns Carr, Ann Courtneidge, Wendy Errol, June Fawcett, James Hadcock, Richard Hoare, Peggy Innos, Gwen Llewellyn, Dionysius MacDuffy, Eric Martin, Jadvige Pelse, Jeanne Steven. Directed by Valery Hovendon. Experience having shown that lunchtime facilities are not required by members, the Club will open daily at 5:30 until further notice, instead of at 12 noon as heretofore."

The original spelling in the manuscript has been maintained—the British spelling of *centre* and *neighbourhood*, and some words perhaps different today, such as *woollen* or *traveller*. Angela Thirkell is known for her original spelling of dialect, and the word *babby* instead of *baby*, for example, is carried over from the original manuscript. The stage directions are provided in bold, a computer feature not available at the time of the typing of the original manuscript.

We have the Angela Thirkell Estate, Serena Thirkell, Literary Executor, to thank for permitting this printing. The estate retains all rights to the work, and any performance of this play requires their permission.

There are also many people in the Society who have made this work possible, and we would like to acknowledge Sylvia Moore and Sue Haley for proofreading and Carol Stone for production, the library at Leeds University, Leeds, England for their special collection archives, and the current board and many others who enable the work of the Society to continue. Our great appreciation also to Andrew Binder of Florida Atlantic University for the cover artwork.

The Good Little Girls is set in France. What were Angela Thirkell's intentions when she wrote this play? We know something of her opinions of the French from the Barsetshire novels, where a French family, the Boulles, rent the vicarage in *Wild Strawberries*. Readers of Angela Thirkell will enjoy the associations—Cadichon the donkey, could have been a cousin of Modestine in *August Folly*. Readers of her other works will see a fascinating range of similarities and differences. For her many enthusiasts, the sudden appearance of an original Angela Thirkell work is an unexpected gift to be greatly treasured. We are enormously grateful to the Thirkell family for this opportunity.

Barbara Houlton
Angela Thirkell Society
North America
2005

The Good Little Girls

A Children's Play in Three Acts
by
Angela Thirkell

This play is founded on four books by the Comtesse de Ségur: Les Mémoires d'un âne, Les Malheurs de Sophie, Les Vacances and Les Petites Filles Modèles.

The time is the eighteen fifties and the scene, the Chateau of Madame de Fleurville, in Normandy.

The clothes should be copied from the illustrations to Madame de Ségur's books.

Characters in the Order of their Appearance

Cadichon	A donkey
Jacques de Traypi	A little boy
Camille de Fleurville)	His cousins
Madeleine de Fleurville)	
Elisa	A maid
Madame de Fleurville	A rich widow, mother of Camille and Madeleine
Madame de Rosbourg	
Gervais	A coachman
Pierre	A gardener
Marguerite de Rosbourg	Mme de Rosbourg's little girl
Madame Fichin	A rich, vulgar widow
Sophie	He step-daughter
A poor woman called Lenormand	
Lucie	Her daughter
M. de Rugès)	
Madame de Rugès)	Sisters and brothers-in-law of Mme De Fleurville
M. de Traypi)	
Madame de Traypi)	
Léon de Rugès)	
Jean de Rugès)	Sons of M. and Mme De Rugès
Médor	A large dog
Lenormand	A sailor, father of Lucie
M. de Rosbourg	Husband of Mme de Rosbourg
Paul	Sophie's cousin
A Robber	

-----oOo-----

THE GOOD LITTLE GIRLS

ACT I, Scene 1

SCENE: *A stable. In the middle are two posts with a manger between them. Before it a donkey lies on some straw. Presently he gets up, stretches himself, and rises. He pulls down the manger which becomes a writing desk, takes out a large pile of paper and a bundle of quill pens, puts on his spectacles and begins to write. There is a knock at the stable door and Jacques de Traypi, a little boy of about seven, comes in. The donkey, without stopping writing, points to an empty box. Jacques sits down and waits. At last the donkey dashes off the last words and lays down his pen.*

CADICHON: The end!

JACQUES: May I talk now, Cadichon?

CADICHON: As much as you like, little Jacques. My great work is finished. **[*He holds up the bundle of papers*]**

JACQUES: Did you write all that?

CADICHON: And lots more.

JACQUES: Oh, Cadichon, how clever you are. You are as clever as — as —

CADICHON: A donkey.

JACQUES: I wasn't going to say donkey exactly.

CADICHON: What else could you say? As clever as a donkey is almost — almost a proverb.

JACQUES: I thought it was as stupid as —

3

CADICHON: Be quiet, sir. You were wrong. I am annoyed.

JACQUES: I didn't mean to be rude

CADICHON: Then I am not annoyed. One might say as stupid as a little boy, but I should not be so rude. Change the subject.

JACQUES: Yes, Cadichon.

[*Silence*]

CADICHON: Change it, then. Don't you want to know something about my great work?

JACQUES: [*Clapping his hands*] Oh, yes, oh yes! What is it about?

CADICHON: About all the children here. About Camille and Madeleine and Marguerite and Sophie and Léon and Jean and Paul and —

JACQUES: — me?

CADICHON: Of course about you, my little Jacques. You always loved me, didn't you, even when the others didn't.

JACQUES: Of course I did, my good Cadichon. I always knew you were a good donkey. Even when you pushed Léon into the —

CADICHON: Change the subject.

JACQUES: Yes, Cadichon.

[*Silence*]

CADICHON: Change it, then. Ask me something else about my great work.

JACQUES: How did you ever find time to write it?

CADICHON: The weather was so bad this winter that I had to stay indoors most of the time. I dislike idleness, so I decided to write down some of the most important events of my life and the

4

adventures I have had since I came to your aunt Madame de Fleurville's house. I flatter myself that my composition has taste and spirit. It may amuse my young friends, and I hope it may teach them that if you wish to be well served you must treat your servants kindly; that people you think stupid are not always so; that kindness will do more than a beating; and that even a donkey has a heart like anyone else to love his masters or suffer from their unkindness, and that even a donkey will revenge himself if he is ill-treated, and be a good friend or a bad enemy.

JACQUES: You were always my friend, Cadichon.

CADICHON: I know, little Jacques.

[*He sheds a tear. They shake hands*]

JACQUES: Will everything be in the book, Cadichon?

CADICHON: [*a little confused*] Not everything — no, not quite. You see, Jacques, I was a very wicked donkey once.

JACQUES : Really wicked?

CADICHON: A perfect devil.

JACQUES: Oh, Cadichon, what a word!

CADICHON: I should not have used it. Change the subject.

JACQUES: Yes, Cadichon.

[*Silence*]

CADICHON: Change it.

JACQUES: I want to know <u>how</u> wicked you were. I can't think of anything else to talk about.

CADICHON: If you insist, I will tell you.

JACQUES: Was it <u>very</u> wicked?

CADICHON: Awful.

JACQUES: Hurrah!

CADICHON: Well, my first mistress used to load me up with eggs and butter and vegetables and cheese and fruit and sit on the top of it all and drive me to the market. And all the way she beat me like a drum.

JACQUES: But that wasn't wicked of you, it was wicked of her.

CADICHON: Wait. One day she tied me up in the market. I was hungry and tired. She never gave me a drink of water or anything to eat.

JACQUES: Poor Cadichon.

CADICHON: And there were the baskets of lovely fresh vegetables on the ground near me, so I ate them all up, and when she came back she was so rude to me and said such dreadful things—

JACQUES: What were they?

CADICHON: I could not sully my mouth by repeating them. Then she began to beat me so hard that I lost my temper and I gave her a kick in the face and broke her nose and two teeth, and then I gave her a kick in the arm and broke her wrist and then I gave her a kick in the stomach. Ha, ha, ha, ha!

JACQUES: Oh, Cadichon, that <u>was</u> wicked.

CADICHON: Yes, I know. It was terrible. But I have repented now. You still love me, don't you?

JACQUES: Of course I do. It wasn't really your fault.

    [*They shake hands*] What happened next?

CADICHON: While the people were looking after my mistress, I ate the rest of the vegetables and stamped on all the eggs, and then I ran away.

JACQUES: Oh!

CADICHON: I lived in the forest till winter came and it was too cold. Then I found a new master. He wasn't a bad sort, but he made everyone work, and I had become lazy and didn't like work, so I hid in a hole covered with bushes. But he set the dogs on me, so I behaved worse than ever. I used to eat the young vegetables. I went into the dairy and drank the cream. I walked on the little chickens and ducks and squashed them. I frightened the children. I bit the pigs. I took the clothes that were hanging out to dry and put them on the muck heap. Ha, ha, ha, ha!

JACQUES: Ha, ha, ha, ha!

CADICHON: [*suddenly becoming serious*] But it was very wicked to behave like that.

JACQUES: Yes, Cadichon.

CADICHON: So I haven't put that part into my book.

JACQUES: [*disappointed*] Oh!

CADICHON: Now I am a reformed character and everyone loves me, so it wouldn't do to put all the wicked things I did into my great work, would it?

JACQUES: No, I suppose not. But I do like to hear about biting the pigs.

CADICHON: Change the subject.

JACQUES: Yes, Cadichon.

[*Silence*]

CADICHON: Change it.

JACQUES: Did you never have any friends then, Cadichon?

CADICHON: Only one. He was the farmer's dog. He was ill-treated himself, but he had a kind heart and used to steal crusts and bring them to me, and we talked to each other about our troubles.

JACQUES: How did you talk?

CADICHON: How did we talk? Why, just as you and I are talking. Children and animals can all understand each other — if the children are little enough. You understand me, little Jacques, but your cousins don't, they are too old. And as for the papas and mammas, they simply look on me as a donkey.

JACQUES: I'll always understand you, Cadichon.

CADICHON: No, little Jacques, you will forget animal language very soon, just like the others.

JACQUES: Never, never. Change the subject.

CADICHON: Yes, let us change the subject. I was telling you about the farmer's dog, the good Médor.

JACQUES: Not <u>our</u> Médor — the one that —

CADICHON: Yes. Your Aunt de Fleurville bought him from the farmer when she bought me, and we were as happy as pigeons in a pie till the dreadful day when — [*He cries*]

JACQUES: Oh, Cadichon, that dreadful day! Must that be in your book?

CADICHON: Yes. That is history.

JACQUES: I don't like history. It is horrible. Poor Médor.

CADICHON: Well, that is all over. And now I am happy and everyone loves me and I have my dear little Jacques to look after me. I am getting old, but donkeys have long lives, and as long as I can stand on my legs I shall serve my little master with all my heart and all my strength and all my intelligence — which is very great.

JACQUES: Cadichon!

[*They embrace*]

CADICHON: Calm yourself. Remember we are men. Shall I begin my story?

JACQUES: Do please.

CADICHON: It begins on a summer day, here in this very garden belonging to your aunt de Fleurville. Your little cousins Camille and Madeleine de Fleurville are playing in the garden —

JACQUES: Where am I?

CADICHON: Wait a little and I'll tell you everything.

[*The stage begins to darken*] It was a beautiful summer day. Your cousins had permission from their mother to go for a walk with their maid Elisa.

JACQUES: The same Elisa that is here now?

CADICHON: The very same Elisa. Now, little Jacques, pay attention and do not interrupt. You must imagine that we are in the garden. Your aunt's house is on one side of us. Then comes the lawn with the little pond and seats under the tree, and beyond the lawn the white railings and the little gate that leads on to the road.

JACQUES: Where is the big gate, the carriage gate?

CADICHON: You can't see it. It is on the other side of the house. Be quiet and listen.

[*The stage is now quite dark*] Your cousins have finished playing with their dolls and are ready to go for a walk. Now listen and you will hear what they are saying. First Camille is speaking......

The garden of Madame de Fleurville's country house. To the right steps lead up to the house which has long windows opening on to a terrace. Centre a tree with seats under it. Left a little pond. Along the back white palings with a little gate. Camille and Madeleine are putting their dolls and toys away. Elisa the maid is sitting sewing under the tree.

[*"Giroflé, Girofla" — Song & dance if required*]

CAMILLE: Now we have put the dolls to bed will you come for a walk with us, Elisa?

ELISA: Of course I will.

[*She folds up her work*]

Which way shall we go?

CAMILLE: Let us go on the high road and see the carriages go by, shall we, Madeleine?

MADELEINE: Oh yes, let us! And if we see any poor beggar women and children, we will give them some money. I have five halfpennies.

[*Mme de Fleurville comes out of the house and looks at them*]

ELISA: Oh, madam, she is a little angel of charity. She gives all her pocket money to the poor.

MME de F.: [*wiping her eyes*] If only their poor father could see them.

CAMILLE: Why do you say <u>poor</u> father, mamma? Papa is in heaven.

MADELEINE: Do not cry, mamma. Papa is with the angels.

MME de F.: Ah, my little angel! Come and embrace your mother.

[*They all embrace*]

ELISA: Little fatherless angels! Kiss your old Elisa!

[*They all embrace*]

MME de F.: Have a pleasant walk, my child. One more kiss.

[*They all embrace. She goes in*]

ELISA: Now, let us go out on to the high road. But look carefully to the left and then to the right, to see that no carriages are coming.

CAMILLE: I hear a carriage.

MADELEINE: The horses are galloping very fast.

ELISA: [*who is looking over the gate*] Good heavens! The horses are running away! The coachman cannot hold them in!

[*Shrieks and tramplings are heard*]

CAMILLE: What is it, Elisa?

ELISA: Merciful heavens! The coachman has fallen off his seat — the wheels of the carriage have gone over him. Do not look!

[*The little girls hide their faces in her skirts*] The ditch! They will all be upset and killed!

[*An awful crash, shrieks, then silence*] Miss Madeleine, I must run for help. I will get the coachman and the gardener. Stay here and play like a good girl, and don't go outside the gate. Gervais!

[*She runs round the corner of the house*]

MADELEINE: I am so frightened, Camille. Will they be dead, do you think?

11

CAMILLE: I expect so. Or have all their arms and legs broken, or their heads come off like our dolls when we drop them.

MADELEINE: I wouldn't mind so much about the people, but oh! the poor horses.

[*She cries*]

CAMILLE: Never mind, Madeleine. If the horses are dead we'll have a funeral.

MADELEINE: Oh yes! And I will help to dig the grave with my spade.

CAMILLE: And we will plant flowers on it and water them every day.

MADELEINE: Where shall we make it?

CAMILLE: Here, on the lawn, in memory of the terrible accident. Let's begin now.

[*They take their spades and begin to dig*]

ELISA: [*at the gate*] This way, Gervais. Carefully, Pierre. Carry the poor lady to the house. No, not like that, stupid. This way. Miss Camille, Miss Madeleine, take care of this little girl while I help to carry the poor lady into the house. She has fainted.

[*She lays Marguerite on the bench*] That's it, Gervais. And then you can go back and help Pierre with the horses.

[*They carry the lady into the house. Camille and Madeleine approach the bench. The little girl has some blood on her forehead and her eyes are shut*]

CAMILLE: Oh, the poor little girl. Help me to lift her, Madeleine.

MADELEINE: I can't. I'm too frightened. Perhaps she is dead. Perhaps her mother is dead. Perhaps the horses are dead.

[*cries*]

CAMILLE: Then I'll lift her myself. If I am not strong enough the angels will help me.

[*She tries to raise the little girl*]

MADELEINE: Let me help you, Camille. I will not be frightened.

CAMILLE: Get some water in your pail, Madeleine, and we will bathe her head. She is breathing. She opened her eyes for a moment.

[*Madeleine runs to the pond with a little pail and gets water*]

And now one of the dolls' counterpanes to wipe her forehead.

MADELEINE: Here you are.

[*She dips the counterpane in the water and wipes Marguerite's face*]

There now, she looks better.

MARGUERITE: Mamma! Mamma!

CAMILLE: Mamma will come in a moment, little girl. Don't cry, Madeleine and I will take care of you.

MARGUERITE: No, no, I want mamma. The wicked horses have run away with mamma.

CAMILLE: The horses haven't run away with your mamma. They fell into a big ditch and mamma went to sleep. When she wakes up you will see her. What is your name?

MARGUERITE: Marguerite.

CAMILLE: And what is your mamma called?

MARGUERITE: My mamma is called mamma.

CAMILLE: But what is her name? She must have a name.

13

MARGUERITE: Of course she has. She is mamma.

MADELEINE: But the servants don't her call mamma, do they?

MARGUERITE: They call her Madame.

MADELEINE: Madame what?

MARGUERITE: No, no, not Madame What, just Madame.

CAMILLE: She is too little to understand.

MARGUERITE: And what are your names?

CAMILLE: I am Camille, and my sister is Madeleine.

MARGUERITE: I shall call you my little mammas. Mamma Camille and Mamma Madeleine.

CAMILLE: Kiss your little mammas then, dear little Marguerite.

[They all kiss]

ELISA: *[coming down the steps from the house]* Ah, the little angels! Miss Marguerite, your dear mamma is much better, but her head aches, so she sends word that you are to play with my young ladies while she rests. Meanwhile I have brought you a tray with some orangeade and some cakes, for you must be hungry and thirsty.

MADELEINE: Dear, good Elisa. Come and have some refreshment with us.

ELISA: I haven't time now. I must go and look after that poor lady. Be good.

[She goes back to the house. Camille pours out the orangeade, Madeleine hands the cakes. While they eat, Marguerite looks at the toys]

MARGUERITE: Oh, what lovely toys! I have never seen such fine dolls. Oh, look at the big doll in bed. And the dolls' house, and the cups and plates! Oh, and a little coach with dolls in it. May I drag it about?

CAMILLE: Certainly, little Marguerite, but not too fast or it will overturn.

MARGUERITE: Now I am the horses. Come along, little coach. Round and round. Now I am trotting. Now I am galloping!

MADELEINE: Take care, Marguerite, it will upset.

MARGUERITE: Round and round, a-gallop, a-gallop.

[*The coach upsets and all the dolls fall out*] Oh, an accident. Oh, I have broken your coach. How sorry I am. [*Cries*]

CAMILLE: Never mind, Marguerite. We will pick up the passengers again and put them in their places.

MARGUERITE: Let me help. Here is a lady with a headache, like mamma. Shall we put her to bed and make her better?

MADELEINE: No, she's only got a wooden head, so it doesn't matter. Now, round we go again, but more gently this time. I will be the postilion and ride in front and blow my horn, and Camille can ride behind with a pistol to shoot the wolves. Off we go.

[*Song "Malborough s'en va-t-en guerre" if required.*]

[*While they are playing, Madame de Rosbourg enters, supported by Madame de Fleurville and Elisa. She is richly but quietly dressed. They lead her to the bench, where she sits. Mme de F. sits beside her.*]

MME de F.: There, my good Elisa, we shall not want you for the present.

ELISA: If you need me, madame, ring the little handbell. I shall be in the young ladies' room, preparing a bed

15

for Miss Marguerite. See how they play together, the little angels!

[*She goes into the house*]

MME de F.:   Repose yourself, Madame. The air is fresh and you are among friends. A glass of orangeade?

MME de R.:   Thank you, Madame. Ah, how grateful I am to the kind Providence that caused my accident to happen at your gate.

MME de F.:   I too, dear Madame, give thanks. I assure you that I feel the liveliest sympathy for you and your little girl.

MME de R.:   Ah, my Marguerite. Come and embrace your mamma, my love.

[*She and Marguerite embrace*]

MME de F.:   Shall I send the children to play in another part of the garden, dear Madame? The noise they make may hurt your head. Camille! You and Madeleine take Marguerite and show her your own gardens. But do not pick any flowers without permission, Marguerite.

CAMILLE: Yes, dear mamma, we will show Marguerite everything.

MADELEINE: She is our little sister, mamma.

[*Mme de Rosbourg wipes her eyes*]

MME de F.:   You feel ill, dear Madame? Another glass of orangeade?

MME de R.:   No, no. It was but emotion at seeing the angelic kindness of your children to my little orphan. Kiss me, dear children.

[*She embraces Camille and Madeleine*]

MME de F.:   And I must kiss your little Marguerite.

[*She embraces Marguerite*]

And now, go and play, my dears.

[*The children go out*]

Dear Madame, you used a word which affected me greatly. You spoke of your orphan child. Has she then no father?

MME de R.:   Alas, Madame, I can hardly say. My beloved husband, Captain de Rosbourg, was lost at sea. My brother, a highly distinguished sailor, who has sailed almost round the world, has made enquiries everywhere, but we have had no news of him, or of the crew or passengers of the fatal ship, the Sybilla. I have withdrawn myself from the world, and live in the country, occupying myself with the education of my only child. Dear Madame, a widow's and orphan's thanks are yours for receiving us today.

MME de F.:   Ah, Madame, you find a sister in misfortune. My husband, a highly distinguished general, was killed in Africa, six years ago, fighting the Arabs. Since then I also have lived alone, devoting my life to my children.

MME de R.:   Your story tears my heart, dearest Madame.

[*Both cry*]

But I fear I trespass upon your hospitality.

MME de F.:   I beg you to say no such thing. I cannot think of letting you go at present in your weak state of nerves. Besides, your coachman and horses are all killed and the carriage broken to pieces, and it will take several days to replace them. Stay with me for the present, and our children shall be like sisters.

MME de R.:   Your kindness, dearest Madame, overwhelms me. I feel that I am indeed among friends. Willingly will I stay with you for a few days, and we can mingle our griefs and share the joys of our children.

MME de F.: Dear Madame, I do not wish to be importunate, but I have one more request to make. We are both widows, both with unprotected children. Our tastes and sentiments are identical. Dear Madame, dear sister, will you not consent to live with us? Why should we separate our children, who are already such friends?

MME de R.: But what would your family think?

MME de F.: I am totally independent of my family, having a large fortune from my late beloved husband. My two sisters with their husbands and children visit me in the summer. Otherwise I am quite alone. Let me persuade you, dear Madame.

MME de R.: I can resist your entreaties no longer, dear Madame. I also have a large fortune and no relatives. I feel already the greatest sympathy for you and your charming daughters. Let us mingle our tears.

MME de F.: Then it is agreed that you stay here for ever?

MME de R.: For ever!

MME de F.: Let us embrace, my sister.

[*They embrace*]

And now to tell our children the joyful news! Elisa! [*She rings the little bell*]

ELISA: [*coming down the steps*] Did you ring, Madame?

MME de F.: Yes, my good Elisa. Go and find the children and send them here. I have to announce to them the good news that Madame de Rosbourg and Marguerite are not going to leave us.

ELISA: Will they live here, Madame?

MME de R.: Yes, Elisa. I have yielded to the prayers of your kind mistress, and henceforward we shall share her home.

ELISA: Oh, Madame, heaven has doubtless sent you to us. Now my dear mistress will no longer be alone.

[She cries]

MME de F.: Your sympathy moves me, my good Elisa. But go and find your young mistresses.

MME de R.: Your warm heart does you credit, my good Elisa. Take this little purse as a reward for your kindness to two unfortunate travelers. And give these pieces of gold to the coachman and gardener who so nobly helped in our rescue.

ELISA: Oh, Madame, it was nothing. Thank you, Madame. *[Curtseys]* I will call the young ladies at once.

[She goes out towards the garden]

MME de F.: I must tell you, dear friend, that I expect a very troublesome visitor today, a Madame Fichini who lives in our neighbourhood. Her husband was a friend of my beloved husband. She is his second wife, and I fear her conduct was partly the cause of his death. She is a vulgar woman and treats her little step-daughter Sophie very harshly.

MME de R.: All that you say interests me deeply in the little orphan girl. Can we do nothing for her?

MME de F.: Alas, I fear not. I would like to adopt the little Sophie and educate her with my children, but as she will inherit an immense fortune from her own mother, the stepmother does not wish to give her up. But here come the children.

[Camille and Madeleine come in]

My dear children, I have some very good news for you. Madame de Rosbourg has promised that she and Marguerite will come and live with us.

CAMILLE: For ever?

MME de F.: For ever, I hope. You, Camille and Madeleine, who are older than Marguerite, must help her by good advice and good examples.

CAMILLE: Indeed we will, mamma. I will teach her how to read and write.

MADELEINE: And I will teach her to put her toys and clothes away tidily.

MME de R.: Little angels! But where is Marguerite? I long to tell her the good news.

MADELEINE: She stayed behind us, to look at our gardens. Here she is.

[Marguerite comes in with her apron full of flowers]

MARGUERITE: Look what I have got for you, Camille and Madeleine. *[She empties the flowers on to the ground]*

CAMILLE: Oh, the poor flowers. They are all squashed.

MADELEINE: You shouldn't put them all in your apron like that, Marguerite. They will die. You funny little girl!

[She and Camille laugh, while Marguerite is more and more perplexed]

[suddenly serious] Marguerite, where did you get those flowers?

MARGUERITE: In your garden.

C & M: In our garden? But you have picked every flower.

MARGUERITE: Yes, and the buds too.

C & M: Oh, Marguerite!

[Marguerite begins to cry]

CAMILLE: My little Marguerite, you heard mamma say you must not pick flowers without permission. Tomorrow is mamma's birthday, and we were going to give her a bouquet of flowers, planted and watered by ourselves. Now we have nothing to give her.

[Marguerite cries]

MADELEINE: We are not scolding you, Marguerite, because we know you did not do it on purpose, but you see how naughty it is not to listen to what mamma says.

CAMILLE: Do not cry, Marguerite. We are not angry.

MARGUERITE: It isn't because you are angry. It is because you are so kind, when I have spoilt your flowers. Please forgive me, I will never do it again. I never meant to do any harm. Mamma, mamma!

[She runs to her mother]

MME de R.: Be as good and forgiving to others, my little girl, as your friends have been to you, and your mamma will always love you. To make up for what you have done, I will send a servant to the town tomorrow and buy a fine bouquet, which Camille and Madeleine shall give to their mother.

MME de F.: Dear friend, you are too good to my children.

MME de R.: Such sweet and forgiving natures as theirs deserve a reward.

MME de F.: And a little girl who so truly repents her faults as Marguerite deserves a reward too. I shall have great pleasure in sending for another bouquet, which Marguerite shall give to her mother.

MARGUERITE: Oh, Madame, how good you are!

MME de R.: Let us all embrace.

> [*Song, "Ah, vous dirai-je, mamman" if required. They all embrace. A bell is heard*]

ELISA: [*coming out of the house*] Madame, it is Madame Fichini and her little stepdaughter.

MME de F.: Beg Madame Fichini to come into the garden, Elisa. Now, my dear friend, you will see the neighbour I was telling you about. Camille and Madeleine, you must be very kind to Sophie, because she has neither father nor mother, and her stepmother is not a good woman.

CAMILLE: I will give her a doll.

MADELEINE: And I will give her a picture book.

MARGUERITE: And I will tell her a story.

> [*Enter Mme Fichini, a large, overblown woman in elaborate toilette, followed by Sophie in a plain cotton frock like a chemise, with a cord round her waist. She is holding her hands over her stomach*]

MME FICHINI: Well, dear Madame de Fleurville, here I am, as large as life and twice as natural.

MME de F.: It is kind of you to visit us. Allow me to present my friend and guest, Madame de Rosbourg.

MME FICHINI: Pleased to meet you. Sophie, curtsey to the ladies. Lower! What's the good of me paying your dancing master a guinea a lesson if you can't curtsey. Take your hands off your stomach, little idiot.

MME de F.: Sophie, my child, go and play with your friends. What a fine toilette you have, Madame Fichini. Really we are hardly suitably dressed to receive you.

MME FICHINI: That's all right, ladies. But if I were you I'd dress a bit smarter. The gentlemen like it. As for my toilette, I always wear any old rag in the country. Who is that little girl playing with your chicks?

MME de R.: She is my daughter, Madame.

MME FICHINI: I shouldn't think you'd have her long — she's too thin. Now then, what are those children quarrelling about?

MARGUERITE: Oh, Sophie, look where you are going. You are treading on the lavender.

SOPHIE: Leave me alone. I want to smell the roses.

MARGUERITE: But you will squash Madeleine's lavender plants. Come off the bed, Sophie.

SOPHIE: Leave me alone, I tell you, idiot!

[Marguerite tries to hold Sophie by the leg. Sophie pushes Marguerite so hard that she falls down. Camille hits Sophie]

MME FICHINI: That's right, Camille! And I'll give her another one, *[boxes Sophie's ears]* the little horror! I can assure you ladies, that if I weren't the sweetest tempered woman alive, I'd beat that child till she bled twenty times a day. Nasty, meddling, quarrelsome brat!

MME de F.: Camille, I am seriously displeased. Did I see my little girl hitting a visitor? For shame, miss!

CAMILLE: Dear mamma, it was very wrong of me, but I could not bear to see Sophie knock Marguerite down.

MME de F.: Sophie was very wrong to knock Marguerite down, but Marguerite should not have pulled Sophie by the leg. She is your guest.

23

MADELEINE: But mamma, Marguerite only pulled Sophie's leg because she was treading on Camille's lavender plants.

[*They all cry*]

MME FICHINI: Yowl! Yowl! What a hullabaloo! I'd whip 'em all and put them on bread and water if they were mine.

MME de R.: I fear, Madame, your methods would give no salutary result. Here we rule by kindness.

MME FICHINI: Pretty kindness!

MARGUERITE: Sophie, I am so sorry I pulled your leg.

CAMILLE: Sophie, I am very sorry I hit you.

ELISA: [*who has come to see what the noise is*] Little angels!

SOPHIE: [*rather sulkily*] Well, then, I'm sorry too, but only sorry to <u>you</u> — not to <u>her</u> [*pointing at her stepmother*]

MME FICHINI: Little toad — what are you saying?

MME de F.: Come, Madame Fichini, we will go indoors and have some refreshments. Sophie can play with the children. I am sure they will all be good now. [*The ladies go into the house*]

ELISA: I will bring you all some more orangeade and cakes, and you can kiss and be friends.

[*She goes into the house and all kiss*]

MADELEINE: Sophie, when you kiss Camille and Marguerite, why don't you put your arms round their necks? They put their arms round you.

SOPHIE: I can't.

CAMILLE: Why not? [*Sophie takes her hands away and shows a great stain on her frock*]

CAMILLE: How did you get that mark on your frock? You came in the carriage.

SOPHIE: It wasn't in the carriage. I got it this morning, when I upset my coffee.

MADELEINE: Why didn't you change your dress to come here?

SOPHIE: <u>She</u> wouldn't let me. She says I get my frocks dirty so often that I am to have cotton frocks, like a chemise, and wear them for three days.

MARGUERITE: But your maid could have washed out the stain.

SOPHIE: She told the maids not to, and they daren't disobey her.

CAMILLE: Poor Sophie!

SOPHIE: Oh, how I wish I could live with you. Does your mother never scold you?

CAMILLE: Never! She knows that if we disobey her and do wrong, we shall be so unhappy that it is punishment enough. Never mind, Sophie. Let us play now. [*Elisa returns with a tray*]

Oh, kind Elisa, how good of you to bring us some more orangeade. Sit down with us.

ELISA: So you think I have time to sit down, Miss Camille? I have all the linen to see to. Now, be good and don't let Miss Sophie get into mischief, or she'll hear of it from <u>someone</u>. [*She goes out*]

MADELEINE: Haven't you any sisters, Sophie?

SOPHIE: No. I did have a dear cousin called Paul, but he was lost at sea, and I do not know if he will ever come back. He was my best friend — after my own mamma died.

MARGUERITE: Poor Sophie. My father too was lost at sea, so you must be a sister to me.

SOPHIE: May I really be your sister?

CAMILLE: You shall be a sister to all of us, dear Sophie, and we will pray for your cousin Paul to come safely back.

MARGUERITE: And for my dear papa.

MADELEINE: And for your papa, little Marguerite.

SOPHIE: But how can I be a sister to you, when you are all dressed so prettily and I have nothing but this dirty old frock? I will wash the stain off in the pond.

MADELEINE: Oh no, Sophie, you mustn't. Mamma forbids us to go near the pond. The water is not clean.

SOPHIE: Well, she isn't my mamma.

MARGUERITE: But Sophie, we must always obey mammas, even when they are not ours. And Madame de Fleurville is so kind. I disobeyed her and picked the flowers, but she didn't punish me, because I hadn't done it on purpose.

SOPHIE: Well, I shall wash my frock and say I didn't do it on purpose.

MARGUERITE: Sophie! Would you tell a lie?

SOPHIE: What a fuss! Wouldn't you tell a lie if you were beaten for telling the truth?

CAMILLE: Our mamma would never beat us for telling the truth.

MARGUERITE: Nor would mine. But I would never tell a lie to her.

MADELEINE: Nor would I to mine.

SOPHIE: Stuck-up idiots! I'm going to wash my dress. Give me your handkerchief, Madeleine. [*She snatches Madeleine's handkerchief and goes to* *the pond and kneels down*] What horrid water! It's all green!

C., MAD. & MARG: Sophie — don't — come away — mamma forbids it — suppose Madame Fichini comes!

SOPHIE: What a fuss about nothing. Now watch me rub my frock. I wish your pond weren't so dirty. I'll have to reach right over to get at some clean water. [*With a shriek she topples over. The little girls run about screaming. Elisa comes rushing out. Pierre, the gardener, comes running with a rake*]

C., MAD. & MARG: Help, help, Elisa! Sophie is in the pond!

ELISA: Here, Pierre, your rake! Quickly, you great booby! [*Pierre rakes about in the pond and catches Sophie by her clothes. She scrambles to land covered with green duckweed. At this moment the three ladies come out of the house*]

C., MAD. & MARG: Mamma, mamma! Sophie fell into the pond!

MME FICHINI: Nasty, ungrateful little horror! [*She shakes her*]

SOPHIE: [*crying*] I was only trying to wash my frock.

MME FICHINI: I'll wash you! Come home, you little wretch! [*She seizes Sophie and beats her with her parasol till it breaks, while the mothers try vainly to stop her and the little girls look on in terror*] Now, miss, come home with me, and it will be bread and water and no clean dress for a week. Well, ladies, you see what a trial the child is. I declare she is driving me into my grave.

PIERRE: [*to Elisa*] Pity she doesn't drive a bit faster.

ELISA: [*to Pierre*] Go along to your work, you great silly — but you're right. [*She pushes him off the stage and goes after*]

MME de F.: Suppose, Madame Fichini, you were to try a little kindness, and reasoned with Sophie. She is good at heart, I am sure.

MME FICHINI: Good at heart? That's a good one! Excuse me laughing, ladies, but you don't seem to see further than the ends of your noses. She drove her father, my late husband, into his grave with her tantrums.

SOPHIE: I didn't! Oh, papa, papa!

MME FICHINI: Get along now, miss. You've disgraced us enough for one day.

MME de R.: But she can't go home in that state. She will catch cold and have a fever.

MME FICHINI: Not she! I'll wrap her up in one of the horse rugs. Well, I don't suppose you'll be wanting to see us again after this little toad's tricks.

MME de F.: On the contrary, I hope you will bring or send Sophie to us as often as possible.

MME FICHINI: If you mean that I'll take you at your word. I'll be glad enough to get rid of her. She eats me out of house and home. Get along, little fright! [*She pokes Sophie with her parasol towards the gate*]

Goodbye, ladies. Goodbye, chicks. And you [*to Mme de Rosbourg*] take notice of what I said about your little girl. Mark my words, she's not long for this world! I know their looks. [*Elisa shows her out*]

MME de R.: Dearest friend, how could you ask that terrible woman to come again?

MME de F.: Because if I quarrel with her, little Sophie will have no friends. Her father and mother were worthy people, friends of my beloved husband, and it is my duty to do all I can for their child. She is good at heart, but if she lives much longer with her stepmother she will become sullen, disobedient, and worst of all, a liar.

MADELEINE: Mamma, I am afraid she _is_ a liar. She told us she would tell a lie sooner than be whipped. That was very dreadful, mamma, was it not?

MME de F.: It should make you reflect, my children, and you too, Marguerite, how lucky you are to have mammas who are never harsh, who reason with you, and by their example show that kindness and truth are your best friends, deceit and cruelty your worst enemies.

C., MAD. & MARG: We are indeed lucky.

MME de R.: So you must all be patient with Sophie, and help her to be good. You, Marguerite, although you are so small, can set an example of obedience.

MME de F.: And you, Camille, must set an example of keeping your temper. I fear that the blow you gave poor Sophie only made her disposition worse. And as for you, Marguerite, you should not have pulled Sophie's leg. Your action made her the more ready to defy you.

C., MAD. & MARG: We will remember.

CAMILLE: When I feel inclined to give way to temper, I will think of Sophie.

MADELEINE: And if I am tempted to act without thinking, I will remember Sophie.

MARGUERITE: And if I am tempted to tell a lie, I will reflect on Sophie's bad example.

BOTH MOTHERS: Dear children.

> [*They all embrace*]

MME de F.:   Now it is getting late, and Elisa will soon be calling you to your supper. Till then, put the toys away and tidy up the flowers that Marguerite dropped. [*To Mme de Rosbourg*] Dear friend, let us sit here and enjoy the evening air.

MME de R.:   I cannot tell you how infinitely peaceful will be to me these summer days spent with you. Days like this, passed in calm reflection from morning to evening, where all breathes in harmony with nature.

MME de F.:   Our life here may be uneventful, dear friend, but who would change the unruffled calm of our peaceful days for the artificial joys of a town?

MME de R.:   How true!

> [*A sound of crying is heard*]

MME de F.:   What is that?

MME de R.:   It sounds like the voice of someone in distress.

MME de F.:   If so, it is our duty to help them. [*Rings*] Elisa!

MADELEINE: [*who has been to the gate*] Mamma, it is a poor beggar girl. May I give her one of my halfpennies?

MME de F.:   [*smiling*] Where are your good resolutions about not acting without thinking, Madeleine? I shall make enquiries, and if the person is suitable, you may give her a halfpenny. More would but encourage her to beg. It shall never be said that I turned from my door any person truly in distress, but one must be careful. Elisa, see who is at the little gate.

ELISA: It is a little beggar girl, Madame. Shall I bring her in?

MME de F.: Yes, my good Elisa.

[Elisa brings in a girl of about fourteen, thin and ragged]

Who are you, my child?

[The girl looks afraid and says nothing]

C., MAD. & MARG: Oh, do not be afraid, poor girl. We won't hurt you. Don't cry.

GIRL : Excuse me, kind ladies, but it is so long since anyone spoke a kind word to me. Some people have set the dogs on us.

CAMILLE: Poor girl, have some cake and fruit.

GIRL: Oh, thank you, kind young lady, but I cannot eat them.

MME de R.: Why?

GIRL : Oh, kind lady, my poor mother is starving. We have eaten nothing but acorns for two days, and I gave the best to her. She was so weak that she lay down on the roadside outside your gate. May I take the cakes to her?

MME de F.: Wait a moment. Elisa, tell Pierre and Gervais to see if the poor woman is outside and bring her in. And get some wine for those poor people. It is our duty, my children, to feed the hungry and clothe the poor. Where do you live, my child?

GIRL : We have no home, kind lady. We wander from place to place. Last night we slept in a ruined hut in the forest. To-day we meant to go to the town where there is a fair, and beg, but my poor mother was too weak.

[Elisa comes back with wine]

31

MME de F.: Here, my child. Drink a little of this wine and eat a cake. We will look after you and your mother.

MADELEINE: Here is a halfpenny, poor girl.

GIRL : Heaven bless you, little lady!

CAMILLE: Here are two halfpennies for you.

GIRL : Oh, you are all too kind.

MADELEINE: Dear Camille, you are more generous than I am. How I admire you.

MARGUERITE: I have no money, but here is my ribbon for you to tie up your hair. Why is it so untidy?

GIRL : Heaven's blessing on you all, young ladies.

[Gervais and Pierre come in carrying a poor woman in rags. They put her on the bench]

MME de F.: Thank you. You can go back to your work. Elisa, give this poor woman some wine.

[The woman drinks, looks round, and says, "Lucie"]

LUCIE: Here I am. Oh, dear mother, heaven has sent these angels to save us. Eat a little cake, dear mother.

MME de R.: See, children, how different is this poor woman from Madame Fichini. She is poor and ragged but she loves her daughter. Let this teach you that virtue can be found in every rank of life.

C., MAD. & MARG: Yes mamma. Yes, Madame.

MME de F.: Where is your husband, my good woman?

WOMAN: I don't know, kind lady.

MME de F.: Has he then deserted you?

LUCIE: Oh, no, kind lady, my father was the best, the kindest of men. But he was a sailor.

MME de R.:   A sailor!

LUCIE: And some years ago he went on a voyage and, oh, ladies, his ship must have gone down, for we have never heard of him again. We were forced to sell all we had and wander as beggars. And what will happen to my poor mother now? How can I support her?

MME de R.:   This story affects me strangely. My child, what was the name of your father's ship?

LUCIE: The frigate Sybilla, kind lady, under Captain de Rosbourg.

MME de R.:   My husband! His ship! Oh, unhappy Lucie, you too are an orphan like my poor Marguerite. Your poor mother mourns, as I do, a husband who will perhaps never return. Have no anxiety for your mother, my child. It shall be my duty to provide for you both.

MME de F.:   And mine, dear friend, to help you in your pleasurable task. The under-gardener's cottage is empty. This very night Lucie and her mother shall be installed there. I will send bedding and all that is necessary in the garden cart. Elisa, go and fetch what is needful, and you, children, may help her.

[Elisa and the three little girls go out]

WOMAN: Oh, kind ladies, this is too much. Ah, ladies, I am sure your kindness will be rewarded and the Captain will return. My poor husband, Lenormand was his name, often spoke of the Captain with tears in his eyes as the best of men.

MME de R.:   We will not lose hope. Heaven has sent you to friends, and we will mingle our prayers for our dear lost ones. I will look out some suitable clothes for you and Lucie, and tonight you will sleep in a good bed and have a bowl of excellent soup.

WOMAN: God bless you, ladies. I am too weak to rise and curtsey, but I assure you of my most respectful devotion. [*She kisses their hands*]

LUCIE: And I will pray for your kind young ladies every day of my life. [*She kisses their hands*]

[*The children coming running in*]

CAMILLE: Good night, dear mamma, Good night, Madame de Rosbourg.

MADELEINE: Good night, dear mamma. Good night, Madame de Rosbourg.

MARGUERITE: Good night, Madame de Fleurville. Good night, dear mamma. Papa will come back soon now, won't he?

MME de R.: We will hope and trust, my child. Good night.

[*The little girls go*]

MME de F.: Elisa will help you to the cottage, my good woman, and I shall visit you tomorrow. Good night, Lucie.

LUCIE: Good night, ladies, and an orphan's blessing on you.

[*Elisa and Lucie help the woman to go out of the garden. It is growing dark*]

MME de F.: Dear friend, permit me to share your hopes that news of the Sybilla may yet be heard.

MME de R.: I hardly dare hope, but I must trust. Meanwhile how wonderfully things have turned out that I and my child should be with you, and that this poor woman was led by Providence to this gate.

MME de F.: Our country life is indeed calm and uneventful, but there are always opportunities to do good for those who wish to take them. Your company will solace me as mine will you and we

34

shall visit the poor woman every day, doing all we can to ameliorate her lot, and experiencing the glow of satisfaction that comes from the consciousness of having performed a charitable action.

MME de R.: Dear friend, we will indeed.

[*They embrace*]

MME de F.: Come, it grows chilly. We will go and visit the children in bed.

[*They rise and go into the house*]

CURTAIN

ACT II

[The same scene, a few weeks later. Mme de Fleurville and Mme de Rosbourg are sewing under the tree.]

MME de R.: How quickly the days pass. I can hardly believe that Marguerite and I have been your guests for six weeks.

MME de F.: Yet it is so. Your companionship, dear friend, has made the hours fly. But today our solitude will be broken. My two sisters, Madame de Rugès and Madame de Traypi, are arriving with their husbands and children. My sister de Rugès has two boys, Léon and Jean. My sister de Traypi has one little boy, Jacques.

MME de R.: I burn to make their acquaintance. It will be pleasant for our little girls to have these young cousins to play with.

MME de F.: The gentlemen will be out shooting a good deal, and will doubtless take the elder boys, Léon and Jean, with them. Little Jacques will stay at home with the girls. I shall give several entertainments while they are here. Today I have invited Madame Fichini to dine and bring Sophie with her.

MME de R.: Ah, dear friend, your patience and kindness with that odious woman astonish me.

MME de F.: It is all on poor little Sophie's account. Have you not noticed that when she is with our sweet children her disposition improves at once? Whereas in her stepmother's presence she at once becomes sullen and defiant.

MME de R.: I applaud your kindness, dear friend, and shall do my best to be civil to Madame Fichini, though I confess her appearance and manners are repugnant to me. But it is our duty to tolerate those less well-bred than ourselves.

[*The children run in*]

[*Song & dance if required: "Il court, il court, le furot"*]

CAMILLE: Mamma, mamma, I have put flowers in our cousin's rooms.

MADELEINE: And I have helped Elisa to make their beds.

MARGUERITE: And I helped to dust the toilet tables.

MME de R.: Now rest a little, my children.

MADELEINE: Haven't they come yet?

MME de F.: Not yet. But they may be here now at any moment. Hark! I think I hear the sound of horses at the front of the house.

[*The children get up in excitement. Elisa comes out of the house*]

ELISA: Madame, the ladies and gentlemen have arrived and are coming into the garden.

[*Enter M. and Mme de Rugès, M. and Mme de Traypi, Léon, Jean and Jacques. The parents are dressed as in the illustrations, with slight exaggeration of the mode. The boys the same. Léon and Jean are about fourteen and twelve, Jacques about seven. A great family greeting and embracing takes place*]

37

MME de F.: And now let me present to you all my dear friend Madame de Rosbourg, who has consented to share my solitude.

MME de RUGÈS: Madame, your devotion to my dear sister has profoundly touched my heart.

MME de TRAYPI: And I, madame, am equally affected, and honoured to make your acquaintance.

MME de F.: Léon, Jean, Jacques, this new little friend is Marguerite de Rosbourg. She has become a sister to Camille and Madeleine, and will be a new little cousin for you.

LÉON: More girls!

M. de RUGÈS: You'll be running <u>after</u> the girls soon, my boy, not away from them.

JEAN: How do you do, Marguerite. I'll take you pickaback if you like. I've got a knife with six blades and a thing for killing pigs.

M. de RUGÈS: You mean well, my boy, but one does not offer pickabacks to girls. That is a sport only fit for boys. And Marguerite is too young to play with your knife.

JACQUES: Will you be my friend, Marguerite, because you and I are younger than the others.

MARGUERITE: With all my heart.

ELISA: Little angels!

LÉON: I say, Camille, we'll have fun these holidays. Do you remember how we caught butterflies last year and how they squirmed when we stuck pins through them?

MME de RUGÈS: Your father and I forbid such cruel sport, Léon. How would you like it, sir, if a giant stuck a pin through you?

JEAN: We'll go birds-nesting, Madeleine. Do you remember when I got a little thrush, and it was dead because I held it too tight.

MME de RUGÈS: For shame, Jean! How would you like it, sir, if a great ogre came and took you out of your warm bed and held you so tightly in his great hand that you were crushed to death?

JACQUES: Don't listen to them, Marguerite. You and I will pick flowers and water the garden.

M. de TRAYPI: You, my little boy, know how to treat a lady.

MME de TRAYPI: To pick flowers and water the garden are very suitable occupations for little girls and boys.

[She kisses Jacques]

MME de F.: And now, my children, I have a surprise for you. Elisa, tell the coachman to bring in Cadichon.

[All the children call "Who is Cadichon?" "What is Cadichon?"]

MME de F.: Wait, and you will see. Cadichon is another new friend. He used to live with a cruel master who made him work very hard and rewarded him with blows and kicks and gave him nothing to eat but grass.

CAMILLE: Grass, mamma? But people cannot live on grass.

MME de F.: Cadichon did, but he got so thin that he was a piteous sight. His coat was thin —

JACQUES: I will give him mine, aunt.

[He begins to take it off]

MME de F.: You are a good and generous child, Jacques, but Cadichon does not need a coat.

MADELEINE: How did he come here, Mamma?

MME de F.: I heard of his story, and bought him.

MARGUERITE: But you cannot buy people, Madame de Fleurville.

MME de F.: You speak without thinking, little Marguerite. I never said Cadichon was a person. You can now see for yourselves, for here he is.

[Gervais leads in the donkey. Shrieks of joy from the children, who all try to get on its back]

GERVAIS: Gently, young ladies and gentlemen. Donkeys can kick, you know. Cadichon is a very good and sensible donkey, but you must treat him well, or he will take his revenge. You must know that he is also a learned donkey.

CHILDREN: A learned donkey? What do you mean? Show us!

GERVAIS: Cadichon, give these flowers to the most amiable lady present.

[He gives a bunch of flowers to Cadichon, who takes them in his mouth, walks around the circle slowly, and presents them to Madame de Fleurville]

CHILDREN: Mamma is best! Aunt de Fleurville is best!

M. de RUGÈS: Your donkey has some sense, my good Gervais.

CADICHON: Of course I have.

[No one but Jacques can hear him speak]

M. de TRAYPI: Permit me, sister de Fleurville, to associate myself with Cadichon's views. *[He bows to her]* Cadichon is a donkey of taste.

CADICHON: Of course I am.

[As before, only Jacques hears him]

40

GERVAIS: Now, Cadichon, here is a piece of sugar. Give it to your best friend.

[Cadichon walks round, looks at everyone and shakes his head]

GERVAIS: Isn't he here?

[Cadichon shakes his head again]

GERVAIS: Where is he then?

[Cadichon looks towards the other side]

Ah, ha, I know who it is. Médor! Médor!

[He whistles. A big dog comes bounding out and jumps on Cadichon, who gives him the sugar]

[Shrieks of joy from the children, who surround Cadichon and Médor and pet them]

MME de R.: You must know, children, that Médor was the watch dog at the farm where Cadichon lived. He also was beaten and starved, so your kind aunt bought him, and now he will be an excellent dog for the chase.

LÉON: I don't think much of donkeys, anyway. I'd like a pony, or a real galloping horse.

[Cadichon looks at him angrily]

CAMILLE: Take care, Léon, you will make Cadichon angry.

LÉON: Pouf! What do I care? He's only a stupid old donkey.

JACQUES: Léon! You should not be so unkind. Cadichon is a good, dear donkey with a soft nose. Aren't you, Cadichon?

[He puts his arm round Cadichon's neck and kisses him]

MME de F.:   Come, sisters, you will want to take off your mantles and bonnets before we dine. What will you do, gentlemen, till dinner is ready?

M. de RUGÈS: We will take our guns and go out for an hour. It will give us an appetite.

[*The ladies go in*]

LÉON & JEAN: Oh, papa, can we go too?

M. de RUGÈS: Why yes, if you like. It is high time you learnt how to handle a gun properly.

JACQUES: I suppose I am too little, Aren't I, papa?

M. de TRAYPI: Yes, dear little Jacques. You shall come when you are older. Meanwhile, stay and take care of your cousins.

MADELEINE: Jacques shall be king today. We will make him a crown of flowers. Come, Camille and Marguerite, we will go and gather them.

[*Song, if required: "C'etait un petit homme"*]

[*The little girls run off. Jacques caresses Cadichon*]

M. de RUGÈS: Now, my boys, are you ready? We will take Médor to pick up the game you shoot.

LÉON: And Cadichon?

M. de RUGÈS: What do you want a donkey for? Donkeys aren't retrievers, my boy.

M. de TRAYPI: Or are you going to chase your game on donkey-back? You'll have to buy Cadichon a pair of wings to keep up with the hares and pheasants.

JEAN: We want him to carry all the game. We shall shoot hares, and pheasants, and perhaps some deer.

M. de TRAYPI: [*laughing*] The idea! Do you think, my poor nephews, that you are going to hit anything?

LÉON: Of course. I have twenty cartridges, and I'll kill at least fifteen animals.

M. de RUGÈS: *[laughing]* That's a good joke. Do you know what you and Jean will kill, my boy?

JEAN: What, papa?

M. de RUGÈS: You'll kill time, and that's about all.

JEAN: Then why do you give us guns, papa, if you think we are too stupid to hit anything?

M. de RUGÈS: To teach you to shoot, little sillies. Nobody hits the first time. When you have missed often enough you learn to hit. Let us get out the guns, de Traypi.

[The two men go into the house]

JEAN: Papa and uncle think we shan't kill anything, Léon, but we will.

LÉON: Of course we will, and much more than they will because we are young and active and can run, and papa and uncle are old.

JEAN: That's true. Papa is forty-two, and you are fourteen and I am twelve. That makes a lot of difference.

[The men come out again with guns, game bags, etc.]

M. de TRAYPI: Come, my boys, are you ready? Here, Cadichon, here is a biscuit for you.

[Cadichon takes the biscuit, walks back to Jacques and puts it at his feet]

JACQUES: Oh, thank you, Cadichon, my own dear donkey.

LÉON: Oh, stop it, Jacques, you little softy.

JACQUES: But Cadichon is my friend.

43

LÉON: Bosh! You can't have a donkey for a friend. You might as well say a pig was your friend.

[Cadichon looks furiously at Léon and walks on his foot]

LÉON: Ow, you great brute.

[He hits at Cadichon. Jacques runs between them and stops the blow. Cadichon gives another horrible look at Léon and walks away]

M. de RUGÈS: Serves you right, my boy. It's time you learnt to treat animals properly. Animals are helpless, and therefore we should protect them and be kind to them, and they will serve us faithfully.

M. de TRAYPI: It was a good act on your part, my little Jacques, to save the donkey from your cousin's blow. Even a little boy like you can set a good example.

JACQUES: I wish Cadichon could stay with me, papa. I love him.

JEAN: Oh, no, we must take Cadichon with us to the chase, papa.

LÉON: We shall really need him, papa.

M. de RUGÈS: Very well, just to show you how foolish you will look when you come back empty-handed. Now, are we ready?

M. de TRAYPI: Léon, hold your gun over your shoulder — so. If you carry it pointed at your friends, you will bring something bigger than game back in your bag.

[Everybody laughs and Léon looks sulky]

M. de RUGÈS: We will take Gervais the coachman with us, because he knows the country. Gervais! Gervais!

GERVAIS: *[Coming in from the side]* Yes, your honour.

M. de RUGÈS: We want you to accompany us for an hour's shooting. You can keep on eye on these young men and lead Cadichon.

GERVAIS: Beg your pardon, sir, but what do you want with Cadichon? He's a good donkey, but he's not trained for shooting.

M. de TRAYPI: These young sportsmen think they will need a donkey to carry their bags.

GERVAIS: Ho, ho, ho! That's a good 'un. Well, young gentlemen, I suppose you must have your way. Come on, Cadichon.

M. de RUGÈS: And we had better have the dog, too, to retrieve for us.

GERVAIS: I'll call him, sir. *[Whistles]* Médor! Médor!

[Médor comes bounding in and the shooting party all go out through the little gate. Léon and Cadichon try to squeeze through together and Léon gets pushed against the gatepost. He tries to kick Cadichon, but Gervais sees it and boxes his ears. As they disappear the little girls come back with some rushes and a wreath of flowers]

CAMILLE: Come, little Jacques, you shall be king today.

MADELEINE: *[bringing a stool]* Here is your throne.

MARGUERITE: And I crown you king.

[She puts the wreath on his head and the bulrush in his hand. The girls dance around him, singing "Frère Jacques". Elisa appears with Sophie, who has on a plain frock and heavy country shoes]

ELISA: Madame Fichini has sent Miss Sophie over to play with you, young ladies. She is coming to dinner herself later. Now, all be good, for I must see to the table.

MADELEINE: Come and rest, Sophie. How hot and tired you look.

SOPHIE: <u>She</u> made me wear my woollen frock and my big shoes. <u>She</u> says I cannot have nice clothes till I am good, and I'll never be good as long as I'm with <u>her</u>.

MARGUERITE: Yes, dear Sophie, with us you are always good. See, this is our little cousin Jacques.

JACQUES: How do you do, Sophie. I am a king. Would you like to be queen?

SOPHIE: Could I?

CAMILLE: Of course you shall. We will make a crown for you. Come, Madeleine and Marguerite, we will go and get some more flowers.

SOPHIE: [*sitting down by Jacques*] I wish I could be a real queen, very beautiful, with silk gowns and golden shoes instead of these horrid great things.

JACQUES: But they are very nice shoes, Sophie. I mean they are nice for the country. They will keep out the wet. And you have a very nice face.

SOPHIE: Have I really? <u>She</u> calls me little horror.

JACQUES: A very nice face. Nearly as nice as Cadichon's.

SOPHIE: Who is Cadichon?

JACQUES: A darling donkey.

SOPHIE: [*crying*] So you think I am a donkey. You are as bad as my stepmother.

JACQUES: Oh no, Sophie, I didn't mean that. Don't cry. I only said you had a very nice face like a donkey, because Cadichon has a beautiful face. You have nice hair too, nearly as thick as Cadichon's.

SOPHIE: I shall be angry if you say I am like Cadichon again.

JACQUES: Very well, Sophie. But you really have very nice, thick hair.

SOPHIE: If only it would curl like Camille's.

JACQUES: Elisa wets Camille's hair and twists it round her finger and then it curls.

SOPHIE: Would mine curl if I wetted it?

JACQUES: Of course.

SOPHIE: I'll wet it in the pond — no, I might fall in again and get wet, and <u>she</u> would beat me. I'll tell you what, Jacques, you water my head with the watering pot, and then my hair will curl.

JACQUES: Yes, Sophie.

SOPHIE: I'll kneel down and pretend to be a flower, and you water me.

JACQUES: What fun. Now I'm the gardener, and I'm going to water the Sophie-flower.

[She kneels down. Jacques sprinkles her with water and they both laugh]

Is that enough?

SOPHIE: I think so.

JACQUES: It isn't curling yet.

SOPHIE: I must twist it round my fingers.

JACQUES: *[while Sophie twists her hair]* I wish I had hair long enough to curl. But they are always cutting it, to make it grow thick, and that stops the curls from coming.

SOPHIE: Does cutting hair always make it thick?

JACQUES: I think so.

47

SOPHIE: Perhaps if I cut my eyebrows they would grow thicker. My stepmother is always laughing at me for having thin eyebrows, and says I'll never get a husband. I'll tell you what, Jacques, I'll take the scissors out of Camille's workbasket and cut them off. Then I'll have fine thick eyebrows and lovely curls, and perhaps my stepmother won't laugh at me so much, and I will have a handsome husband who will take me away from her.

JACQUES: But, Sophie, you mustn't play with scissors. It is forbidden.

SOPHIE: No one will see. Come behind the bushes and watch me and then I'll cut yours.

JACQUES: No, no, you mustn't.

SOPHIE: All right, cry-baby. Just come and see me cut mine.

[*She drags him off. The ladies come into the garden from the house*]

MME de RUGÈS: [*to Mme de Rosbourg*] I must thank you again, dear madame, for your kind attention to my sister de Fleurville. I assure you she looks ten years younger since she has had a friend to share her life.

MME de R.:   I know only too well, dear madame, that no friend can replace a sister, but I am only too happy if I can mitigate Madame de Fleurville's solitude.

MME de TRAYPI: [*to Mme de Fleurville*] Dear sister, I cannot tell you how glad I am that your charming friend, Madame de Rosbourg, has promised to stay with you. I was often sad, thinking of you all alone in the country with your two little girls, but now you have a sister.

MME de F.: Madame de Rosbourg is indeed very dear to me, sister, but no one can fill in my heart the place that you and my sister de Rugès occupy.

MME de R.: [*to Mme de Traypi*] Dear madame, how charming a child is your little Jacques. What a delightful companion he will be for my little Marguerite.

MME de TRAYPI: I have done my best, dear madame, to teach him to be good and obedient, and to think of others. Your little Marguerite will set him an excellent example.

MME de F.: Marguerite is a very amiable little girl. And what a pleasure it will be for all three little girls to have such fine young men as Léon and Jean to play with.

MME de RUGÈS: I only hope that my two boys will not be too rough for the little girls. Schoolboys are not always as polite and considerate as one would wish.

MME de R.: But they have good hearts, dear madame, and what more could a mother desire?

[*All the ladies sigh. Lucie appears at the little gate and comes timidly forward*]

MME de F.: Here comes our little protégée. Come forward, Lucie, and curtsey to these ladies.

[*Lucie makes a curtsey*]

MME de RUGÈS: Who is this interesting child?

MME de F.: Her father, a sailor, was lost at sea. She and her mother, homeless and foodless, were sent by a kindly Providence to my gate and now live in the under-gardener's cottage.

LUCIE: And every day my poor mother and I bless the ladies who are our benefactresses. [*to Mme de*

Rosbourg] Pray, madame, is there any news of the Sybilla?

MME de R.: Alas, no, my child. But we must not lose hope. Tell your worthy mother that I am sending down some nourishing broth for her this evening.

LUCIE: Oh, madame, you are too kind. Pray excuse my intrusion, ladies, but my mother, though much stronger, is not yet fit to walk alone, so she sends me daily to enquire for news. Thank you and bless you, kind ladies.

MME de F.: Let me tell you, my sisters, that Madame de Rosbourg's husband was captain of the frigate Sybilla, which must have perished with all hands, for nothing has been heard of her for two years.

MME de R.: And Sophie's cousin Paul was also on that fatal ship, so there are here three families mourning their dear ones. Ah, ladies, if you had but known my beloved husband!

LUCIE: Ah, ladies, if you had but known my dear father!

MME de F.: And to think of Sophie's cousin Paul — only a boy — being lost with so many other gallant hearts in the depths of the raging sea!

MME de RUGÈS: It tears my heart.

MME de TRAYPI: I can but weep in sympathy.

[*They all weep*]

MME de F.: But I hear the voices of the gentlemen. They have not been long at the chase. Let us recompose ourselves, my dear friends.

[*MM. de Rugès & de Traypi come in and salute*]

MME de RUGÈS: You are soon back, my dear.

M. de RUGÈS: It was confoundedly hot, and those boys of ours were such a nuisance that we left them with Gervais.

MME de F.:   Allow me to ring for some refreshments.

[She rings]

M. de TRAYPI: I only hope the youngsters won't shoot each other — or Gervais.

[All the ladies scream]

MME de TRAYPI: My husband exaggerates. But I do not think they will shoot even a sparrow.

[Elisa comes in]

MME de F.:   Elisa, bring some wine and cakes to refresh the gentlemen, and some orangeade for the children. Where are they?

ELISA: In the garden, madame. At least, I saw our young ladies picking flowers, and the others will not be far off. And excuse me, madame, but Madame Fichini's carriage has just turned into the drive. Do you wish her to come into the garden?

MME de F.:   Yes, my good Elisa.

[Elisa goes out]

My sisters, I am sorry to inflict this neighbour on you. She is insupportably vulgar, but I take an interest in her little stepdaughter, Sophie, she whose cousin Paul was lost in the Sybilla, and therefore must be civil to the stepmother.

[Enter Madame Fichini, more sumptuously dressed than ever, followed by Elisa with a tray of refreshments, which she places on the table. Pierre, the gardener, sweeps up leaves at the side]

MME de F.:   Good day, Madame Fichini. Allow me to present my sisters and their husbands.

[A very formal presentation takes place with bows and curtseys]

They are paying me a visit of some weeks. Their boys are also with us.

MME FICHINI: Always pleased to see new faces. Don't you find the country a bit dull, ladies?

MME de R.: Oh no, madame! With the changing panorama of nature ever before one, how can one be dull for a moment.

MME FICHINI: Well, I dessay your young people will be getting into plenty of mischief. All boys need the birch. It sweetens the blood, as I say to my Sophie when I beat her.

MME de F.: Brother de Rugès, pray give a chair to Madame Fichini and we will have some refreshment.

[*M. de Rugès brings forward a chair. Mme Fichini sits down with such a swirl of skirts that she knocks the chair over and falls on her back. The company can hardly keep from laughing. Pierre the gardener bursts into a guffaw and Elisa boxes his ears. The gentlemen rush to Mme Fichini's aid and with difficulty get her upright again*]

MME de RUGÈS: A glass of wine to restore you, madame.

MME FICHINI: A glass of wine, indeed! Some people think fine words butter parsnips. Oh, you can all laugh at me, but if I have broken my leg it will be no laughing matter. Give me another glass of wine. What is that great, clumsy oaf of a gardener laughing about? If he were mine I'd make him laugh on the other side of his mouth.

[*Elisa, stifling her giggles, pushes Pierre away*]

Fine feathers make fine birds, I daresay, but I don't think much of you stuck-up gentlefolks. I could buy

52

all your dresses as easy as you'd buy a turnip. Fill that glass again, young man.

[*Jacques comes running up to Mme de Traypi in terror*]

JACQUES: Mamma, mamma! Don't let her cut off my eyebrows.

MME de TRAYPI: Calm yourself, my little Jacques. No one will hurt you.

JACQUES: It is Sophie, she is coming after me with the scissors. Mamma, mamma!

[*Sophie comes running in, brandishing the scissors. Her hair is standing on end in wet tufts, and her eyebrows have gone*]

MME de F.: Sophie, my child, what is the meaning of this?

MME de RUGÈS: Gad! The little girl has cut her eyebrows off. Well, you are a sight, miss.

[*The company cannot help laughing*]

MME de R.: Give me the scissors. Sophie, what is the meaning of this?

MME FICHINI: [*rising*] You wicked little good-for-nothing, what have you been up to now, making a laughing stock of us all?

SOPHIE: Nothing, madame.

MME FICHINI: I'll nothing you. Come, miss, out with it.

JACQUES: Elisa wets Camille's hair to curl it, so Sophie told me to water her hair with the watering pot.

M. de TRAYPI: You might as well water bean sticks to make them curl, my boy.

JACQUES: And cutting people's hair makes it thicker, so she cut off her eyebrows to make them grow, and she wanted to cut off mine. Mamma, mamma!

[Mme Fichini takes a birch rod from under her shawls]

MME FICHINI: So you thought you could defy me, miss, in front of your kind friends. Well, I've got an old friend of yours here, and he will have a word to say to you.

[She chases Sophie, catches her, and is beginning to thrash her when the gentlemen catch her by the arms and take the birch]

Very well! Call yourselves gentlemen, do you? I've seen better ones made of potato peelings. Come here at once, miss. I'll take you home, and there you'll stay. No more gadding about for you if this is how you behave.

SOPHIE: Please forgive me. I didn't mean to. It was only to be beautiful like Camille and Madeleine.

MME FICHINI: Beautiful! Who is going to look at a little toad like you, with no eyebrows. Come along, I say.

MME de F.:   Madame Fichini, may I beg you to reflect. Sophie has been very foolish, but she is not wicked. At least you will let her visit her little friends again when she has told you that she is sorry.

MME FICHINI: Well, I won't, and that's flat. I've put up with enough in this house. Come along, Miss Baldface.

[She seizes Sophie, who screams]

MME de F.:   Once more, I implore you, be merciful.

MME FICHINI: *[throwing Sophie off, who runs to Mme de Rosbourg's arms]* You've implored once too often, my fine lady. Keep the little brat. If she stays here now, she never comes back to me. Now, pay your money and take your choice.

MME de F.:   Sophie, you have heard what your stepmother has said. Reflect well. Will you go home with her, or stay here?

SOPHIE: Will you have me? I am so naughty. Nobody wants me. Oh, I will be good, I <u>will</u> be good.

[*The sisters and brothers-in-law say confusedly "But reflect, dear sister", "You do not know what you are doing", "What will people say?", "Such an ill-bred child, my love"*]

MME de F.:   Our children shall decide.

[*The little girls come running in with flowers*]

My children, Sophie has been very naughty and disobedient, and her stepmother has punished her severely. She must either go back with Madame Fichini and never come here again, or stay here and never go back to Madame Fichini. Which shall it be? Marguerite shall speak first, because she is the youngest.

MARGUERITE: If Sophie is unhappy, let her stay here, because here no one is unhappy.

MADELEINE: If Sophie comes to live with us she will learn the habits of obedience and truthfulness that you, dear mamma, have always taught us.

CAMILLE: We shall treat her as our sister, and in setting her a good example we shall improve our own characters.

[*The ladies, except Mme Fichini, begin to wipe their eyes*]

MME de RUGÈS: Sweet angels!

MME de TRAYPI: Dear loves!

MME de F.:   There is one who has not spoken. What does little Jacques think?

JACQUES: If you won't cut my eyebrows off, Sophie, you can stay for ever and ever, because you have a nice face.

M. de TRAYPI: Bravo, my boy, you have a generous nature.

MME de F.:   You have heard what your little friends have to say, Sophie. Now, make your choice.

SOPHIE: Oh, please, please let me stay with you all.

MME FICHINI: All right, ladies, I wish you joy of the nastiest little creature I've ever met. Don't trouble to send her back, because I won't have her. I'm going to marry a fine new husband, a Russian Count, and he won't want the brat. As for her fortune, don't think you'll get it. Goodbye, everyone. I never liked you, and now you positively make me sick, you pack of....umbrellas.

[She goes majestically out]

MME de F.:   Elisa, take Miss Sophie upstairs, wash her, and make her tidy, and find a frock of one of your young ladies that will fit her.

[To Sophie, who is endeavouring to thank her]

That is enough, my child. Go with Elisa, and when you are fit to be seen, you may return.

[Elisa takes Sophie away]

MME de TRAYPI: You have taken a great responsibility upon yourself, sister, but heaven will reward you.

M. de RUGÈS: Gad! The old girl looked a sight when she fell down. The little gal looked a sight too, with no eyebrows!

MME de F.: Come, let us have some refreshment. Children, hand the wine and cakes to your guests again.

MME de RUGÈS: I wonder where Léon and Jean are. It is getting late.

M. de RUGÈS: They are sure to be back for their dinner, my dear.

MME de TRAYPI: I thought I heard a shot a few moments ago. They must be nearing the house.

[Gervais appears at the gate. He is leading Cadichon, who has a sack across his back with something in it]

MME de F.: Ah, here is Gervais. Come in, my good Gervais. Well, how did the chase go?

GERVAIS: Not too well, madame.

MME de R.: The boys aren't hurt, are they?

GERVAIS: I wish they were, saving your presence, ladies and gentlemen, the young varmints!

M. de RUGÈS: Well, they seem to have made a few hits. You have brought back a fine bag of game.

GERVAIS: You may well say a fine bag, sir.

[He takes the sack off Cadichon and opens it]

It is Médor, the best of the dogs, Mr. Léon shot him, by mistake for a partridge. I told him again and again to look out, but he wouldn't take any notice. Poor Médor was retrieving one of my birds, sir, and Mr. Léon fired straight at him — that's all.

M. de RUGÈS: Médor! Little fool! I wouldn't have had this happen for a hundred pounds. I shall never let Léon carry a gun again.

[The boys are seen at the gate]

Come in, sir. What have you to say for yourself?

LÉON: I don't know why you are so cross, papa. People often shoot dogs by mistake.

M. de RUGÈS: Shoot dogs? By mistake? Where did you hear that?

LÉON: Oh, everyone knows that even great sportsmen often shoot their dogs.

M. de RUGÈS: Ladies! Gentlemen! I must ask you to forgive me for having brought such a conceited dunce as Léon to the house. Go indoors at once, sir, and put your gun in my room. You will not see it again till you have learnt some sense. Now you will see the result of your stupid conceit and obstinacy. As for you, Jean, you have been lucky enough to do no harm, but may the lesson be a warning to you.

LÉON: But, papa —

M. de RUGÈS: Silence. Not a word more, or my cleaning rod will have a word to say to you.

[Léon goes sulkily indoors. Meanwhile Gervais has taken Médor out of the sack and stands holding him in his arms]

MME de F.: You must bury poor Médor, my friend. Dig a grave for him near the stables, and the children will plant flowers on it in memory of their friend.

[Gervais goes sadly out with Médor's body. The little girls follow. Cadichon, who has been eyeing Léon with rage, has slunk away into a corner and is not noticed. The company go slowly into the house, except Jacques, who remains in the background. On the steps of the house Mme de Fleurville pauses and calls "Pierre"]

PIERRE: Yes, madame.

MME de F.: Pierre, go and help Gervais to dig a grave for poor Médor, and I will send a bottle of wine for you both when the ceremony is over.

PIERRE: Yes, madame. Thank you, madame. Excuse me, madame.

MME de F.: Well?

PIERRE: I thought I'd better tell you, madame, to tell the young ladies and gentlemen to keep away from the pond. It had got very dirty, and I had to drain the water away today, and it's all nasty mud. I will fill it tomorrow morning early.

MME de F.: Thank you, Pierre. I will tell them.

[She goes into the house. Pierre goes to the stable. Cadichon comes out and stands dejected, his head drooping. Jacques creeps up to him and fondles him]

JACQUES: Poor Cadichon. I am so sorry.

CADICHON: Thank you, little Jacques.

JACQUES: Médor was your special friend, wasn't he?

CADICHON: Yes. When I was a poor overworked donkey at the wicked farmer's, he was my only friend.

JACQUES: Cheer up.

CADICHON: I can't. When I think that Médor used to find food for me when he was half-starved himself — and get beaten for doing it too.

JACQUES: Don't cry.

[He wipes Cadichon's eyes]

CADICHON: And then your aunt de Fleurville bought us both and we have been as happy as the day is long. We had long talks in the stable every night, and told each other everything.

59

JACQUES: Poor Cadichon.

CADICHON: I knew some misfortune would happen when that horrible Léon came. I hated him at once. He is cruel, rude and insolent.

JACQUES: Hush, Cadichon.

CADICHON: I won't. He is a murderer. Gervais told him again and again never to fire when Médor was in front of the guns. He disobeyed. I saw what had happened and galloped up, just in time for my dear friend to give me a last wag of his tail.

JACQUES: Oh, Cadichon, how dreadful.

CADICHON: And then, little Jacques, I had to carry Médor home on my back.

[*Silence*]

But I'll be revenged if I have to wait twenty years. I'll split his skull with my hoofs and tear him to pieces with my teeth!

JACQUES: Cadichon, you must not speak like that. It is wicked. We must forgive our enemies.

CADICHON: Perhaps men must. But I am an animal — only a donkey, as Léon said — it doesn't matter for me.

JACQUES: But Cadichon, I shall be very unhappy if you hurt Léon. You are my friend, and I cannot bear to hear you speak so wickedly.

CADICHON: You can't understand, little Jacques.

JACQUES: Cadichon, please be good. Léon didn't do it on purpose.

CADICHON: What difference does that make? No, little Jacques, I must revenge my friend or perish in the attempt.

[*Elisa is heard calling Jacques*]

JACQUES: Elisa is calling me, Cadichon. I must go in. Please be good, because I love you.

CADICHON: Will you always be my friend?

JACQUES: Always.

CADICHON: Whatever I do?

JACQUES: Yes...whatever you do.

[He goes sadly into the house. Cadichon goes back among the bushes. Léon comes out, looking sulky and ashamed]

LÉON: What a fuss about a dog. And I didn't <u>mean</u> to shoot him. Papa goes on as if I were a murderer.

[Cadichon has got between him and the house]

Hullo, donkey!

[Cadichon advances on him, showing his teeth]

Go away, you stupid ass!

[He throws a stone. Cadichon rears on his hind legs and strikes at him with his forefeet. Léon backs towards the pond]

Here, go away. Get out, I say! Get out! Help! Help!

[Cadichon presses him backwards till with a scream he falls into the pond. Cadichon gives a loud bray of triumph and dances about in glee. Pierre and Gervais come running in at the noise]

PIERRE: Why, what is Cadichon doing in the garden?

LÉON'S VOICE: Help! I'm suffocating!

GERVAIS: It is Mr. Léon in the pond. It'll do him good to swim.

PIERRE: But I drained it today. It is all mud. Quick, Gervais, call everyone while I get a pole.

[Gervais runs up to the steps, calling "Fire!" "Murder!" "Thieves!" Pierre comes back with a long pole and holds it out to Léon, who emerges

black with mud from head to foot just as the whole house party come out into the garden]

MME de RUGÈS: Léon! Oh, heavens!

[*She faints*]

M. de RUGÈS: Léon, what the devil are you doing?

LÉON: Cadichon pushed me into the mud.

M. de RUGÈS: And what were you doing to him?

LÉON: Nothing.

M. de RUGÈS: Come, sir, the truth.

LÉON: I only threw a stone at him.

M. de RUGÈS: Then it serves you right. I was going to beat you, sir, for your behaviour today, but this is punishment enough. Don't come any nearer, sir. You stink! Gervais, take Mr. Léon to the stable-yard and pump on him.

GERVAIS: Yes, sir. With pleasure.

[*He leads Léon away*]

MME de F.: Pierre, Cadichon must be severely beaten for this.

PIERRE: Yes, madame.

JACQUES: [*Throwing his arm round Cadichon's neck*] No, no. Do not beat him. He pushed Léon into the pond because Léon had shot Médor, and Médor was Cadichon's greatest friend.

PIERRE: It is true, madame, that Cadichon and Médor were always together. Quite an understanding they seemed to have.

MME de F.: But this is ridiculous.

JACQUES: Oh no, aunt. Cadichon told me so himself.

M. de TRAYPI: My dear little Jacques, donkeys can't talk.

JACQUES: But Cadichon can.

M. de TRAYPI: You are very fond of animals, my dear little boy, and doubtless you think you understand them, but to say that Cadichon <u>told</u> you what he did is ridiculous.

JACQUES: Pray, aunt, do not let Cadichon be beaten.

MME de F.: Well, Jacques, as you forgave Sophie for frightening you with the scissors, I will forgive Cadichon. But in future the children must not ride him unless a grown-up person is present, for he is, I fear, a vicious, unreliable animal, whom no one can love. Pierre, take the donkey to his stable.

M. de RUGÈS: I think a glass of brandy before we dine—

M. de TRAYPI: By all means.

[They go inside]

MME de F.: *[to Mme de Rugès]* Are you quite recovered, dear sister? Léon will be none the worse, I assure you.

MME de RUGÈS: Yes, I am myself again. But the shock was terrible.

MME de R.: Let us sit quietly here till the dinner bell rings. Yet another long peaceful day has passed.

MME de TRAYPI: Yes. How calm indeed is country life; how soothing.

MME de RUGÈS: No incidents to break its even course. All is tranquil.

MME de F.:   One day follows another, each with its little round of duties and pleasures. No shocks disturb the mind, and nature lays her soothing hand on our minds and hearts.

[*The dinner bell rings*]

Come, dear friends, let us go in.

CURTAIN

ACT III, Scene I

The same scene, later in the holidays. Sophie and Marguerite are weaving baskets of rushes. Jacques is watching them, and handing them the rushes. They are singing as they work. "Savez vous planter les choux." When they have finished their song there is a silence and Jacques sighs.

MARGUERITE: What is the matter, Jacques?

JACQUES: I am so unhappy.

MARGUERITE: But why? You have a papa and mamma, and everyone is kind to you and loves you.

JACQUES: It is about Cadichon.

SOPHIE: Cadichon is a bad donkey. No one loves him since he pushed Léon into the pond.

JACQUES: Oh no, Sophie, he isn't bad. He was angry because Léon had shot Médor, but now he is truly sorry that he behaved so badly.

SOPHIE: How do you know?

JACQUES: He told me so.

SOPHIE: Jacques, you are a silly little boy. Cadichon can't tell you anything. He is only a donkey.

JACQUES: But he does tell me, Sophie.

SOPHIE: All right — cry-baby!

MARGUERITE: Sophie, do not be unkind to Jacques. Dear little Jacques, you must not invent such stories, for they are not true. Look, my basket is finished.

JACQUES: Oh, how pretty!

MARGUERITE: Would you like it?

65

JACQUES: Oh, thank you, Marguerite.

[He dances about, crying "My lovely, lovely basket!" Camille and Madeleine come in with a big basket of cherries]

CAMILLE: Look what we have picked! Mamma says we may eat some, and the rest we may make into jam. The cook will help us.

SOPHIE: Hurrah! We'll eat it all for supper.

MADELEINE: We must give some to Lucie's poor mother.

SOPHIE: It is too good for a poor beggar-woman.

CAMILLE: Why should it be too good for Lucie's mother if it isn't too good for us? You should not speak like that, Sophie.

SOPHIE: Why not? Do you suppose Lucie's mother is used to having jam?

MADELEINE: It is just because she isn't used to it that we shall give her some of ours for a treat.

SOPHIE: She can eat bread and cheese. I shan't bother to make jam for a poor old woman.

MARGUERITE: We shan't ask you to help us, Miss Stuck-up. We don't want you to help us. Camille only invited you to join us in a kind action because she has such a good heart.

SOPHIE: Well, some of those cherries are mine, and I'm going to eat them myself.

MARGUERITE: None of them are yours, no one gave them to you. But I'm not so greedy and selfish as you, so you can have mine. There you are!

[She takes handfuls of cherries and throws them at Sophie. Sophie hits her. Madeleine holds Sophie while Camille holds Marguerite]

CAMILLE: Marguerite! What are you doing?

MARGUERITE: Oh, Camille, how wicked I have been, I am so sorry that I lost my temper and threw the cherries at Sophie. Please forgive me, Sophie.

SOPHIE: Let me go, Madeleine. I'm going to give Marguerite a hit for every cherry she threw at me. Let me go, or I'll hit you too.

[*She shakes Camille off and rushes on Marguerite, just as Mme de Fleurville, Mme de Rosbourg and Elisa come out. Mme de Fleurville without saying a word takes Sophie by the arm and leads her to the bench*]

MME de F.:   Sophie, you will go to your room and write out a hundred times, "I have been a naughty girl."

SOPHIE: But it wasn't me, it was Marguerite.

MME de F.:   Silence. You will then have your dinner alone, and go to bed.

SOPHIE: It's all Marguerite's fault. I hate her. I won't go, I won't go.

MME de F.:   Elisa, take Miss Sophie to her room. Give her pens, paper and ink, and leave her alone.

[*Elisa drags the unwilling Sophie away*]

MME de R.:   Marguerite, I am shocked and ashamed.

MARGUERITE: I am very sorry, mamma.

MME de R.:   You will go to your room and remain there till I give you permission to come out.

MARGUERITE: Yes, mamma.

[*She begins to move towards the house*]

CAMILLE: Madame de Rosbourg, Marguerite wanted to give the cherry jam to Lucie's mother, and Sophie said jam was too good for poor people. Sophie was very naughty to say that.

MME de R.: Sophie may have behaved very badly, but Marguerite should not have lost her temper. She has no excuse, for she has been better brought up than poor Sophie, and should have set her a good example. She should have explained to Sophie that we must always help those who are poorer than ourselves.

CAMILLE: But Sophie wouldn't listen.

MME de R.: Sophie has a quick temper and has been badly brought up, and never taught to be charitable, but she has a good heart, and if you had all spoken seriously to her, she would have repented her words and become better. Now she is angry and sullen.

MADELEINE: Mamma, please let me go and speak to Sophie. I am sure she is crying, and very unhappy and sorry.

MME de F.: No, Madeleine. I wish her to remain alone for the present, till she is truly sorry.

[A noise is heard. Elisa comes running out, her apron covered with ink]

ELISA: Madame! Ladies! Miss Sophie has gone mad. She threw the inkstand at me, and bit and scratched till I couldn't hold her.

[Sophie appears on the steps. She throws a bundle of pens at the company, shouting, "Here are your old pens!" Then she comes down the steps, tearing her copy book to pieces and throwing the paper about, shouting, "Here's your stupid old paper! I won't write, I won't, I won't!" Mme de Fleurville rises. Jean comes in.]

JEAN: Hullo! Sophie, is this a paper chase? I say, you are in a temper. What's up?

SOPHIE: I hate you!

[She takes off her shoe and throws it at him]

MME de F.: Come here, young lady.

SOPHIE: I hate you all.

JACQUES: *[running up to her]*

You don't hate me, Sophie, do you?

SOPHIE: *[throwing her other shoe at him, hitting him on the forehead]*

Yes I do. I hate you all. You are all pigs.

[An awful silence falls. Camille and Madeleine run to pick up Jacques and console him]

CAMILLE: Oh, my poor little Jacques, what a big bump on your forehead.

MADELEINE: And your poor little knee is grazed. Oh, Sophie, how could you?

[Sophie bursts into tears and kneels down by Jacques]

SOPHIE: Oh, Jacques, I never meant to hurt you. Forgive me, Jacques, please forgive me. I'll never be naughty again, never, never!

JACQUES: You aren't naughty, Sophie. It was only the shoe. Poor Sophie.

[He puts his arms round her and kisses her. Everyone cries.]

MME de F.: My good Elisa, please pick up these papers and pens and go and change your apron. Sophie, my poor child, what have you to say for yourself?

SOPHIE: Oh, I am so unhappy. Please forgive me, and I will never be naughty again. I have been a wicked, disobedient girl and you have all been angels. You and Madame de Rosbourg, and Camille and Madeleine and Marguerite, and little Jacques and Elisa. Please, please make me good!

69

MME de F.:   Sophie, your behaviour has been so shocking that I am almost in despair. Your sincere repentance and promises of amendment deserve pardon, but you cannot mix with your friends till you can command your temper. You might have killed little Jacques. You have thrown an inkstand at the good Elisa. You have fought with Marguerite. For all this you are forgiven, but you must be punished all the same.

SOPHIE: [*kissing her hand*]

Oh, madame, your kindness touches me deeply. Your pardon and the pardon of all my friends is all I ask. I deserve my punishment richly. I will return to the house and beg Elisa's pardon, and then I shall apply myself to writing out the words "I have been a naughty girl," not one hundred, but two hundred times.

MME de F.:   Go, Sophie. And may your repentance, this time, be lasting.

[*Sophie curtseys and goes indoors*]

My children, let this be a lesson to you all. Remain as I have taught you to be, good, obedient and unselfish, and you will not only be happy but the cause of happiness in others. You may see in Sophie that pride, selfishness, and disobedience make you unhappy and bring unhappiness to all around.

CHILDREN: Yes, mamma. Yes, aunt.

MME de F.:   Now, to efface this painful impression I will give you a piece of good news. Lucie's mother is so much better, thanks to the assistance I have been able to give her, that the doctor permits her to go out. I have therefore sent Gervais to the cottage with Cadichon to bring her here, so that she may express her thanks to us for all our kindness.

CHILDREN: Oh mamma — aunt — madame — how good you are!

MME de F.: Here they come.

[Gervais comes in, leading Cadichon with the poor woman on his back, accompanied by Lucie. He assists her to dismount, ties Cadichon up. Jacques runs over to caress Cadichon]

MME de F.: Do not go near the donkey, little Jacques. He might bite, or kick.

[Jacques sadly goes back to his place, waving kisses to Cadichon, who waves a kiss back]

My poor woman, how do you feel?

WOMAN: Thanks to your kindness and this good lady's *[motioning to Mme de Rosbourg]*, I am now nearly well. My first wish has been to thank you for all you have done for me and my little Lucie.

MME de F.: As soon as you can walk, I shall find some position for you in which you can earn enough for your small needs. Lucie shall enter my household and be trained by my excellent Elisa. Who knows but she might become a lady's maid for one of the three young ladies.

LUCIE: Oh madame! A lady's maid to one of these dear young ladies! My heart will break with joy.

MME de F.: You see, children, if you do good to the poor you will be rewarded by the gratitude of sincere and pious hearts.

WOMAN: Pray, ladies, is there any news of the Sybilla?

MME de R.: Alas, no. But I shall never give up hope.

MME de F.: In honour of your recovery, my good woman, we will have a little feast. Madeleine, tell

71

Elisa to bring us some lemonade and cake, and some wine.

MADELEINE: Yes, mamma.

[She goes out]

CAMILLE: Poor woman, will your husband bring Marguerite's papa back?

WOMAN: Oh, my blessed, innocent young lady, who can say? I pray daily that the good Captain and my dear husband may be restored to us, and the young cousin of Miss Sophie too.

[Léon comes out with Madeleine. As he passes, Cadichon makes a snap at him]

MME de F.: Come Léon. Where have you been? We have seen very little of you lately.

LÉON: I have been carrying potatoes, aunt.

CAMILLE: Carrying potatoes? But you are a gentleman.

LÉON: Even gentlemen may have to earn money.

MADELEINE: But why do you want money, Léon? Your papa and mamma give you everything you need.

LÉON: I wanted something special, and the market gardener in the village pays me sixpence a day if I help him to carry the potatoes from the field to his cart. No gentleman need be ashamed of honest toil.

MME de F.: I do not like mysteries, Léon. What is all this story of sixpences?

LÉON: Aunt, please do not think me rude or ungrateful if I do not tell you. I have a very special reason.

MME de F.: Well, Léon, I shall not interfere. Your own parents must judge. Are they aware of what you are doing?

LÉON: No, aunt. But I shall tell them, as soon as —

MME de F.:   Enough. I do not wish to pry into your secrets. But notice, my children, that a secretive nature is rarely beloved, while a frank and open nature is loved by all. Serve the refreshments, Elisa.

[Jacques pulls Léon aside]

JACQUES: Léon, Don't be unhappy. I won't ask you why you want the money, but I love you.

LÉON: Dear little Jacques, I will tell you if you promise to keep it a secret from everyone. I am earning money to buy a new dog to replace Médor. The keeper has one which he will sell for five shillings. Today I have earned the last sixpence, and he is to send me the dog. Poor Cadichon, I killed his best friend. Perhaps if he has a new friend he will understand how sorry I am and no longer hate me.

JACQUES: May I tell Cadichon?

LÉON: Yes, you funny little boy. He won't understand.

JACQUES: *[earnestly to Cadichon]* Cadichon, do you know what Léon is doing? He is working every day to earn money and buy a new Médor, because he is so sorry for what he has done.

CADICHON: Money won't make Médor alive again.

JACQUES: Cadichon, you must be generous. Poor Léon is very, very unhappy, because you don't love him.

CADICHON: Jacques, you are a good little boy, and you are right. I will forgive Léon. And I admit that I was wrong to push him into the mud. I must lose my pride and learn to be humble and affectionate.

JACQUES: Dear Cadichon! May I tell Léon?

CADICHON: No, little Jacques. Before long I hope to find some way of showing my repentance.

[The fathers and mothers come in]

M. de RUGÈS: Well, Léon my boy, we haven't seen much of you lately.

MME de F.:   Léon is full of mysteries, my brother. I do not wish to hint that anything underhand is going on, but I do not feel confidence in him.

M. de RUGÈS: What is this, my boy?

LÉON: There is a mystery, papa. But if I give you the word of a Frenchman that there is nothing wrong in it, will that satisfy you?

M. de RUGÈS: If you give your word, my boy, that is enough.

[*They shake hands, much moved*]

M. de TRAYPI: Well, here we all are. Your healths. [*He drinks*]

MME de TRAYPI: All except Sophie. Where is she?

MME de F.:   I was obliged to correct her, and she is at present writing out an imposition.

MME de TRAYPI: Doubtless she will benefit by it.

MME de RUGÈS: And where is Marguerite?

MME de R.:   I was obliged to correct her, and she is at present in her room

MME de RUGÈS: Doubtless it will do her good.

M. de RUGÈS: Come, sister de Fleurville and Madame de Rosbourg, the holidays are nearly over, and we must be gay. What about pardoning these two young ladies?

MME de F.:   I cannot but consent to your request, my brother. Elisa, you may tell Miss Sophie to come into the garden.

MME de R.:   I can refuse you nothing. My good Elisa, have the kindness to tell Marguerite that she also is free.

ELISA: With the greatest pleasure, my good ladies.

[*She goes out*]

MADELEINE: Mamma. There is someone at the gate.

MME de F.: Who is it?

CAMILLE: A poor man, mamma. He looks hot and tired, and I am sure he is hungry. May he come in?

M. de RUGÈS: He can go round to the kitchen door and get something to eat. We can't have all the tramps in the neighborhood hanging around the gate. There have been some unpleasant characters about lately. There was a robbery not far off last night, so Gervais tells me, and all the people in the house were murdered.

[*All the ladies scream*]

MME de R.: With you and M. de Traypi here, and those boys of yours, we have nothing to fear. May I beg that the poor man may come in and have some wine. I feel that my poor husband, if he escaped from the fatal shipwreck, may have been glad of bread from a charitable hand.

M. de RUGÈS: [*aside*] And gladder still of wine, I'll be bound. What do you say, sister de Fleurville?

MME de F.: Madame de Rosbourg's sentiments are mine. Madeleine, you may tell the poor traveller to come in.

M. de RUGÈS: Your sentiments do you honour, ladies, but you'll find yourselves in trouble if you let every tramp in the neighbourhood get into the garden.

MADELEINE: Poor man, come in and rest.

[*The man comes in. He is quite obviously a shipwrecked sailor, with striped jersey, sea- boots, a parrot, and a bundle*]

MAN: Thank you, little lady. It's many a day since a kind voice spoke to me.

MADELEINE: Come here, and I will bring you some wine.

MAN: Wine's too good for the likes of me, miss. However, if you say so, I'll drink it and welcome.

[*He pulls his forelock to the company*]

Servant, ladies and gentlemen.

MME de R.: If, as I gather from your appearance, you are a sailor, nothing is too good for you, my man.

MAN: That's very good of you, mum.

[*Madeleine brings him wine. Marguerite comes out of the house*]

MME de R.: Marguerite!

MARGUERITE: [*running up and kissing her mother*]

Yes, mamma.

MME de R.: Give that poor man a cake. He may be hungry.

MAN: Marguerite? Begging your pardon, mum, for being so familiar, but it's a name I know well. Often did my brave captain speak of his little Marguerite at home. Well, if she was as pretty as you, miss, she was a good 'un. No offense.

MME de R.: Your captain? Marguerite? Tell me, good man, what was his name?

MAN: de Rosbourg, mum and as good a captain as —

MME de R.: Ah!

[*She faints*]

MARGUERITE: Mamma! Mamma!

MAN: What's up? I hope I haven't said nought as I oughtn't. Sure as my name is Lenormand —

WOMAN: [*who has been sitting quietly with Lucie in the background till now*] Ah!

[*she faints*]

LUCIE: Mother, mother! Speak to your Lucie!

MAN: Lucie? Why shiver my timbers if it ain't my little Lucie!

LUCIE: Are you...no...yes...

MAN: Yes, my girl, here I am, your own father. And there you are, as large as life and twice as natural. Give us a kiss, my girl.

LUCIE: Father!

[*They embrace*]

Mother! Mother! See, it is father!

WOMAN: My husband!

[*They embrace*]

MME de F.: [*who has been attending Mme de Rosbourg*] How are you, dear friend?

MME de R.: It is nothing. I am well again. It was emotion. Good man, I am Madame de Rosbourg, and this is the captain's little girl.

MAN: Well, shiver my timbers, here's a go! I'm an old sea-dog, mum, but it makes me cry like a babby to see my good captain's lady and his little girl — a picter she is too.

MME de R.: Have you no news of the captain, my man?

MAN: No, mum. Never set eyes on him since the shipwreck. We got ashore on a raft, him and me and Mr. Paul — a fine upstanding young man that was on the ship along with us — and the savages got us, and I never see'd them again. I escaped and got to a port and worked my passage home, but I'll be bound the savages ate the Captain and poor Mr. Paul.

MME de R.:   Ah!

[*She faints again*]

[*While the ladies are attending to her, Sophie comes out, bearing a large copy book. She is exquisitely dressed, and her eyebrows have grown again*]

SOPHIE: Here is my imposition, Madame de Fleurville.

[*she holds up a book with large writing*]

And now I shall never be naughty again. Kind Elisa has put on this pretty dress for me, and see, my eyebrows are now thick and handsome!

MME de F.:   Dear child, you are indeed reformed, and I am sure that for the future you will be as good as Camille, Madeleine and Marguerite.

SOPHIE: With your help, my kind protectress, I shall endeavour to be even better. But who is this man?

MME de F.:   Providence has sent to our gate the husband of the poor woman whom we assisted, the father of Lucie.

SOPHIE: How glad I am that Lucie has her father again. From her I shall learn that patience has its reward. And has Marguerite's Papa come back too?

MME de R.:   [*recovering from her swoon*] It is nothing. Only a slight emotion. No, Sophie, my beloved husband has not returned, but I feel a calm certitude that he will. Heaven, which has sent this poor sailor back to his wife and child, cannot fail to restore a Captain to his sorrowing spouse and daughter.

MME de F.:   And a cousin to our dear Sophie, we hope.

ELISA: Excuse me, ladies, but two gentlemen are at the door. Their carriage has broken down, and they ask if they may rest here till the wheelwright can be fetched.

MME de F.:   Ask them to join us, Elisa. On such a day all are welcome. We must share our joys with others, as we would help them to bear their griefs.

[*M. de Rosbourg and Paul enter, followed by Elisa. Mme de Rosbourg does not see them at first*]

Gentlemen, be welcome.

M. de R.: Madame, you are hospitality itself. May I trespass on your kindness so far as to ask if you know where a Madame de Rosbourg lives. I believe it is this neighbourhood.:

MME de F.:   Sir, you need to go no further. There she is.

M. de R.:   My wife!

MME de R.:   My husband!

MARGUERITE: Papa! Papa!

M. de R.:   My little Marguerite.

[*They all embrace. General rejoicing*]

M. de R.: Sophie, why do you not rejoice like the others? Why are you crying?

SOPHIE: Because while everyone is happy, I am alone. If only my dear cousin Paul were here. If only I could hear his voice.

PAUL: [*putting his hands over her eyes*]

Guess who is here?

SOPHIE: Paul! [*She flies to his arms. Everyone cries*]

M. de RUGÈS: Silence, everyone. Now I shall propose a toast. Health and happiness to our newly restored friends!

M. de TRAYPI: And may the sun of prosperity ever drive away the clouds of adversity.

[*Everyone drinks*]

MAN: Captain, you ain't forgotten me, have you?

M. de R.: Lenormand, my honest friend!

MAN: And Mr. Paul, if I may make so bold, where is he, sir?

PAUL: Don't you know your old friends, Lenormand?

MAN: Bless me, it's you, sir. Growed out of all knowledge! As handsome a young man as ever I wish to set eyes on. You'll be breaking all the young ladies' hearts, sir.

WOMAN: Now then, husband, that's enough of your sea ways. Remember there's quality here.

MAN: No offense to the company.

M. de R.: We can make every allowance for you, my good Lenormand, on this joyous occasion.

M. de RUGÈS: Tell us, Captain, how you escaped.

M. de R.: I am only a plain sea captain, but I will tell you as best I can. After the shipwreck this good fellow Lenormand, with Paul and myself, took to a raft and managed to make an island.

PAUL: You do not say, my good protector, that on the raft you covered me with your coat, and gave me your last drop of water.

[Murmurs of "how noble"]

M. de R.: Spare a sailor's modesty, my boy. Any Frenchman would do the same.

PAUL: On landing, we were overpowered by savages, who carried poor Lenormand away. My benefactor and I were taken to their chief, several days' march away.

M. de R.: You do not say, Paul, that you gave me your own shoes when mine were worn out, and carried my bundle when I was overcome by fatigue.

PAUL: One does not mention these things. Any French youth would succour the weak, and how could I neglect one to whom I owed my life?

[*More murmurs of "noble youth"*]

M. de R.:   The savages treated us kindly. We taught them to dance and sing, and say the alphabet.

PAUL: You do not say, Captain, that you saved their chief from a puma at the risk of your own life.

M. de R.:   No, my boy. Modesty forbids.

PAUL: Then, ladies, at last a French vessel appeared. Bidding farewell to the kindly savages, we embarked for our beloved France.

M. de R.:   He does not tell you, ladies, that we were attacked on the way home by pirates, whom he beat off single-handed.

PAUL: No Frenchman could do otherwise. I shall treasure to my dying day the scars that testify to my feeble efforts on behalf of one to whom I owe life and liberty.

[*He opens his shirt and shows terrific scars. The ladies hide their faces and scream. More murmurs of "Noble, generous youth"*]

M. de TRAYPI: Well, that's all very fine. It must be nearly dinner-time, sister de Fleurville. I daresay the gentlemen are hungry.

M. de R.:   Before we go in, let me announce to you that I shall take the first opportunity of buying a property in this neighbourhood. Lenormand, you and your wife and child shall be taken into my service.

MME de R.:   And it shall be my care to fit Lucie to be maid to Marguerite.

[*The Lenormands fall on their knees and kiss their benefactors' hands*]

81

SOPHIE: What will you do, Paul?

PAUL: I have no fortune, Sophie. I shall go to sea again and make my way from powder monkey to admiral. Whenever I return on leave I shall visit you here, if Madame de Fleurville will permit me.

MME de F.:   This house will be your home, Paul, whenever you wish to come, as it is Sophie's now.

[Mme Fichini appears at the gate. She is pale and thin and poorly dressed and carries a jewel case. She totters in and looks around timidly]

ALL: Madame Fichini!

[Sophie runs to Mme de Fleurville]

MME FICHINI: Do not run away from me, Sophie. I do not wish any harm to you.

MME de F.:   But what has happened? Have you had an accident? Can we be of any assistance?

MME FICHINI: Ladies, you are too kind, but no one can help me. I have made my own bed and must lie on it. My husband is not a Russian Count but a wicked imposter, who has ill-treated me and spent all my money. I have nothing left but these rags and this casket of jewels. My house and estate are to be sold tomorrow.

[Murmurs of compassion]

And worse than that, I fear he is a criminal. He has been out a great deal at night lately, and whenever he comes home late there has always been a robbery or a murder in the neighbourhood. What shall I do?

SOPHIE: Madame, I have sixpence left from my last week's pocket-money. It is all I have, but here it is.

[She gives it to Mme Fichini]

MME FICHINI: Can you forgive me for all my unkindness, Sophie?

82

SOPHIE: Yes, indeed, with all my heart.

MME FICHINI: You are a good girl, Sophie. I was a bit hasty sometimes, but forgive and forget is what I say. And I'll tell you something, my girl, your fortune is safe in the bank, where my wicked husband can't get at it. And now, goodbye.

[She totters away, wiping her eyes]

M. de R.: Wait! I will buy your house and estate. What do you ask?

MME FICHINI: It cost me ten thousand pounds.

M. de R.: I offer you one thousand.

MME FICHINI: I accept. My benefactor!

[He counts the money into her hand]

MME de F.: And I, madame, as Sophie's guardian, will buy your jewels on her behalf.

MME FICHINI: Here they are. They cost twenty thousand pounds.

MME de F.: I offer you two thousand.

MME FICHINI: You are too kind, too generous.

[Mme de Fleurville counts the money into her hand]

Now, goodbye. With this money I shall go to another part of the country and live a humble and virtuous life, hoping that my cruel husband will never find me. Goodbye, Sophie.

SOPHIE: Goodbye, stepmother.

[Mme Fichini goes out]

Now that I have my fortune, shall I be able to give money to the poor?

MME de F.: Your question, dear child, shows me how completely your disposition is changed. Thanks to

the influence of Camille, Madeleine and
Marguerite, you are now a perfect character.

SOPHIE: How can I ever thank you enough, dear
madame, and you Madame de Rosbourg, and you,
my dear little friends.

PAUL: Alas, Sophie, the poor sailor lad is now further
from you than ever.

SOPHIE: Half my fortune, dear Paul, shall be yours.

PAUL: Sophie, I cannot disappoint your generosity. I
accept.

M. de R.:   I'd have done the same in your place, my boy.

MME de F.:   Now, we will all go to dinner.

[*They all go towards the house. M. de Rugès
speaks to Léon*]

M. de RUGÈS: Léon, you had better lock the garden
gate. If there are thieves and robbers about, we don't
want them here.

[*He goes out. Night draws on. Léon remains
behind, reflecting*]

LÉON: Now everyone is happy but myself. Oh, what can
I do to show that I am truly sorry for my evil
behaviour? If only the keeper would send the dog
soon, I could perhaps make Cadichon forgive me.
But it is too late now. He will not send him tonight.

CADICHON: Poor Léon, how cruelly I misjudged him!
Alas that I cannot tell him that I understand what he
says, and am willing to be his friend.

[*While Léon and Cadichon are plunged in
dejection, a hideous thief creeps in through the
gate, which Léon has not locked. Léon looks
round and is going to call for help when the thief
puts his hand over his mouth and draws a knife.
Just as he is about to stab him Cadichon breaks*]

his tether and rushes at the thief, shakes him, knocks him down, stamps on him, and brays at the top of his voice. The whole party rush out and the coachman and gardener rush in with lanterns]

M. de RUGÈS: What's this?

M. de TRAYPI: Cadichon! A man on the ground!

M. de RUGÈS: My sister, you should get rid of this donkey. He is vicious.

JACQUES: No, papa, he isn't!

LÉON: Father! Cadichon has a nobility that shames me. I had not carried out your command to lock the gate. This man crept in and attempted to murder me. Cadichon, though I had killed his best friend, sprang to my rescue. He has saved my life.

PAUL: Noble donkey! He has saved us all from death.

GERVAIS: Beg pardon, gentlemen, but I know that man. He's a regular bad lot. He's the one as said he was a Russian Count and married Miss Sophie's poor stepmother. He broke into a house and got away with all the money and jewels only last week and murdered all the people. The police'll be glad to see him. Come on, you. Pierre, give us a hand.

[They remove the man]

LÉON: Cadichon, I am your friend for ever. Can you forgive me?

[Cadichon nods. He puts out his foot and he and Léon shake hands. A loud barking is heard, and a large dog, exactly like Médor, bounds onto the stage and licks Cadichon's nose]

This dog, dear parents and friends, I bought with the money I have earned by carrying potatoes. He is to replace Médor, as a hunting dog, and as a friend for Cadichon.

[loud applause]

M. de RUGÈS: You have a noble and generous soul, my boy.

PAUL: I am proud to know you, Léon. I would have done just the same in your place.:

LÉON: It is nothing. No French boy could do otherwise.

M. de TRAYPI: Well, what about our dinner? It will be getting cold. Come along.

[They all go in except Jacques. It is now quite dark]

JACQUES: Dear Cadichon, I am so happy. Now everything is all right, and we are all friends. I knew you were good all the time.

CADICHON: You never forsook me, little Jacques.

JACQUES: Never. You are my dear Cadichon, and we will always be friends and tell each other our secrets.

CADICHON: You will get bigger, little Jacques, and forget animal language. But I shall never forget you, never, never.

[The stage is now quite black and fades into the last scene]

ACT III, Scene II

When it lightens again we are in the stable. Cadichon is sitting at his desk and Jacques *asleep in the straw. Cadichon lays down the last sheet of paper and looks at Jacques. Then he puts his papers in a large envelope and addresses it TO THE PUBLISHER in such large writing that the audience can see it. He sticks the envelope in a notch between the bars of his manger, folds up his writing desk, and lies down in the straw near Jacques. A noise is heard outside. The little girls come in, calling Jacques, who wakes up and looks round*

JACQUES: Cadichon was telling me a lovely story.

SOPHIE: You've been dreaming, little Jacques.

JACQUES: It was real, wasn't it, Cadichon?

   [*Cadichon brays. All the children laugh*]

   [*puzzled*] I can't understand him.

CAMILLE: Of course you can't. He's only a donkey, though a noble and unselfish one.

MADELEINE: Wake up, Jacques. Mamma has prepared a great feast, and there are to be jellies and ices and orangeade and sugar plums, and afterwards we shall dance.

MARGUERITE: And there will be a feast for the poor people with food suitable for their station.

   [*The boys come in*]

LÉON: Hullo, Jacques, there you are. We have been looking everywhere for you. There is to be a surprise for Cadichon.

PAUL: Cadichon is a noble animal. I would have done exactly the same in his place.

JEAN: Cadichon, you are a brick.

[*The fathers and mothers come in, followed by the Lenormands, Elisa, Gervais and Pierre*]

MME de. F.: What is that envelope on Cadichon's manger?

PAUL: [*taking it down*] It is addressed To The Publisher.

M. de RUGÈS: It is the sacred duty of all Frenchmen to post letters which they find lying about. I shall post it.

[*He takes it from Paul*]

M. de TRAYPI: No Frenchman would willingly defraud a paternal government by sending a letter unstamped. I shall stamp it.

[*He takes it from M. de Rugès and affixes an enormous stamp to it*]

PAUL: Generous man! I should have done exactly the same myself.

MME de F.: And now, my children, before we go to the feast there is a little ceremony to perform. Elisa, bring the wreath.

[*Elisa brings forward a great wreath of flowers*]

MME de F.: Brother de Rugès, as Cadichon saved your son from the thief, will you crown him in the name of the whole company.

M. de R.: Pardon a rough sea-captain, madame, but no Frenchman can allow another to carry out a public duty when he is capable of doing it himself. Allow me —

[*He lays hold of the wreath*]

PAUL: Pardon me, my benefactor, but sooner than see one to whom I owe my life performing so noble a task, I will do it myself.

[*He lays hold of the wreath*]

SOPHIE: Madame de Fleurville, please let Jacques do it.

MME de F.:   You are right, my child. Jacques, crown your friend.

[*Jacques puts the wreath over Cadichon's head and kisses him. Médor comes bounding in. Everyone shouts, dances, and sings. Gradually they go out of the stable, dancing. Jacques goes out last, blowing kisses to Cadichon*]

CADICHON: Goodbye, goodbye.

JACQUES: Dear Cadichon, he is braying for joy.

[*He runs out, and Cadichon lies down on the straw and goes to sleep*]

THE END